Endorsements for *Together*

"Copeland and Gilliland have brought us Together, and we do well to give it a close read. They are powerfully and boldly testifying to serving Lovers Lane UMC, a microcosm of our larger global denomination in its diversity and missional passion. Together witnesses to the best of our relevant Wesleyan Evangelical heritage."

Bishop Mike McKee
North Texas Annual Conference, The United Methodist Church

"As I read *Together*, Eph. 4:1-6 runs in the background, '…bearing with one another in love, making *every effort* to maintain the unity of the Spirit in the bond of peace.' Having served a highly diverse congregation, Copeland and Gilliland are a living testimony to what is possible when we make every effort to maintain the unity of the Spirit."

Bishop Cynthia Fierro Harvey
Louisiana Annual Conference, The United Methodist Church

"This may be the most important book United Methodists read this year. Written from a pastoral heart, it represents the plea of countless pastors of vital congregations where Christ's witness is thriving through a unity in diversity that is 'hard-won and grace-drenched.' It is hopeful, positive, and generous, recognizing the diversity of churches and contexts and the need each has to learn from the others."

Dr. Lovett H. Weems, Jr.
Distinguished Professor of Church Leadership, Wesley Theological Seminary

"I want all the restrictions specifically about homosexuality eliminated from the Discipline of the United Methodist Church. I expect my wish is to be frustrated. Short of that, the One Church Plan is the best compromise we have, and this book by Copeland and Gilliland is the most compelling and heart-felt iteration of that moderate position I have seen. But regardless of one's stance on this issue before the United Methodist Church, I recommend a careful reading of this book's argument and proposals."

Dr. Tex Sample
Robert B. And Kathleen Rogers Professor Emeritus of Church and Society, The Saint Paul School of Theology

"Lovers Lane has met with its own theological and socio-political issues and conflicts in our history, as noted in this book. Ultimately, we have prevailed through uniting around a common mission: loving ALL people into relationship with Jesus Christ. *Together* is a living testament that there is a solution that can work for United Methodists who share a unity of purpose and focus. Pastors Copeland and Gilliland have effectively planted a seed for thought in support of unity in diversity and in the One Church Plan, which I fully embrace."

Scott Williams
Chairman, Staff-Parish Relations Committee, Lovers Lane UMC

"Many communities of faith talk about unity and oneness but it's hard to deny that Sunday mornings are commonly the most segregated time of the week. Lovers Lane United Methodist Church belies that norm, working hard to put hands and feet to words of faith. *Together* tells of our congregation and the unity we have developed as a body of Christ. Though no group is perfect, the work of uniting people in LLUMC is a great start! Congratulations to Dr. Stan Copeland and Rev. Scott Gilliland for a phenomenal book describing a phenomenal church."

Hon. Tina Yoo Clinton
Member, Board of Stewards, Lovers Lane UMC

TOGETHER

TOGETHER

United Methodists of the Temple, Tabernacle, and Table

Stanley R. Copeland and Scott Gilliland

TOGETHER
UNITED METHODISTS OF THE TEMPLE, TABERNABLE AND TABLE

ISBN 978-0-692-19041-8 (paperback)

Library of Congress Control Number pending

All scripture quotations unless noted otherwise are taken from the New Revised Standard Version of the Bible, copyright 1989 by the Division of Christian Education of the National Council of the Churches of Christ in the United States of America. Used by permission. All rights reserved.

Excerpts from *Lord, He Went, Remembering William H. Hinson*, by Stanley R. Copeland are © 2006 by Abingdon Press, used by permission. All rights reserved.

Excerpts from *Staying at the Table: The Gift of Unity for United Methodists,* by Scott Jones are © 2008 by Abingdon Press, used by permission. All rights reserved.

Excerpts from *Credo,* by William Sloane Coffin are © 2004 by Westminster John Knox, used by permission. All rights reserved.

Excerpts from *"Inclusivism, Idolatry and the Survival of the (Fittest) Faithful,"* by Dr. William Abraham, in *The Community of the Word: Toward an Evangelical Ecclesiology* are © 2004 by Intervarsity Press, used by permission. All rights reserved.

Front Cover Photography by Keri Lynn Lucas
Cover Design by Chris Denney and Michelle Dekkers

Printed in the United States of America
First Printing September 2018

Published by Colinasway LLC
3000 Custer Rd. Suite , Plano, TX,

Dedicated to

Claire Marie Copeland
Our first and only grandchild who was born on January 21, 2018.
I pray that we United Methodists will be true to our baptism vow
and nurture her in the faith of the open Table,
where grace abounds, and all are welcome by Jesus
who calls us together.
- SRC

Andie Jane Gilliland
Our daughter, part toddler, part dinosaur.
For reminding me that there is always someone younger than me
watching how I lead, listening to what I preach,
and wondering if I notice them, too.
I pray she experiences not only the Church's imperfections,
but also, its beauty, its grace, and its love.
- SG

And a special "Thank You!" to

Lovers Lane United Methodist Church and the leadership of the Board of Stewards, Staff-Parish Relations Committee, and staff for your inspiration, encouragement, and support. *Together* was literally written "together" and the words in these pages come from our faith community.
Joan McKee, for being the first to read *Together* and saying, "publish it."
Deborah Ackerman, for her first edits and giving us a "thumbs up."
Neil Alexander, Paul Franklyn, and a collection of publishing professionals who came around us and offered their expertise.
Rev. Kalaba Chali for authoring the Forward and being a beloved friend.
Rev. Don Underwood for your contributions through interview and writing that greatly enhanced our work.
A generous anonymous donor whose contribution made it possible for us to literally give away thousands of books, and **the other financial backers** who gave so that others all over the world could read *Together*.
Finally, to the **Uniting Methodists** movement, whose spirit of graciousness with followers and critics has been an inspiring example of the best of our denomination's love and prayer for unity.

Contents

FORWARD

By: Rev. Kalaba Chali

Sometimes books are written for academic purposes and we try to make them be practical. Other books are written for practical ministries, but prove difficult to bring into the classroom for reflection. This book does both in blending practical experience in a local church context with theological reflection and balanced rationale, causing one to think and hope for a United Methodist Church being united in mission. When Stan called and asked me to write to write the Forward to *Together*, I was simply excited to hear from my former pastor and mentor. After reading the book, I count it an honor to be asked.

Stan is the person who helped me in my first full-time pastoral appointment in the United States, and through our ministry at Lovers Lane God did some amazing things in our midst that none of us were quite prepared for and all of us were richly blessed by the ministry God created. I served as the Pastor of Outreach from 2007 to 2010 in this large congregation, with a particular focus on our growing Heart of Africa[1] ministry and an incredible weekly prison ministry. I have experienced firsthand the possibility of being "One Church" in the midst of diversity at Lovers Lane.

On a personal note, my wife Jill and I were married at the church. Ours was the first wedding in the new Shipp Chapel, and Stan was one

---

[1] "Heart of Africa" is a worship fellowship at LLUMC. Their members are largely refugee immigrants from West Coast and Central African nations.

---

of the officiants. He also came to St. Louis to baptize our daughter and preach to our Missouri congregation. So, professionally and personally, Lovers Lane and Stan Copeland are connected to our family and we know so well the blessing of being "together."

I have known the Reverend Scott Gilliland as a gifted young preacher and pastor, and now I have experienced his witness through his excellent writing. Scott represents one of a dozen (or more) young persons at Lovers Lane who are hearing God's call on their lives, entering seminary, and pursuing ministry in the United Methodist Church. His insights, particularly as one from his generation, are important to listen to and hear with open minds and hearts.

Together is indeed a book of hope. The hope is extended to our United Methodist family, which is going through discernment to determine how we can live together and engage in God's mission from different perspectives and life experiences. This book raises the context of a real-life United Methodist church community that makes diversity work along the lines of theological, cultural, socioeconomic, and yes, sexual orientation. Together gives us a tangible example of ministry "together" as a powerful possibility.

I believe the story of Lovers Lane helps other churches by giving us tangible examples of how we can find unity in our diversity. As a Zambian pastor who has served on this American church staff at Lovers Lane, I can personally attest to these experiences. As Copeland and Gilliland discuss in the book, Lovers Lane creates space for both economically challenged and economically flourishing people; one may be given a bulletin at the door by a millionaire and sits down in the pews beside a former incarcerated person.

In addition, for our African sisters and brothers who serve as delegates to General Conference, this book offers an example of how Africans from Liberia, Kenya, Burundi, Congo (DRC), Cameroon, Zimbabwe, Sierra Leone, and other countries feel right at home in a congregation where there are persons who identify themselves socio-politically and theologically as conservatives, liberals, and those in between. All these persons have one thing in common: they love Jesus and are working together "loving ALL people into relationship with Jesus Christ."

As a person who has lived and worked in various countries, serving at Lovers Lane was energizing to me. Lovers Lane reminds me of my experience at Africa University (AU) in Zimbabwe, probably the only place where one can live the "African" experience. Like Lovers Lane, this United Methodist-related institution, AU, is place where United Methodists live out their unity in diversity and get an opportunity to practice what heaven will look like. Just like on the AU campus where every day is a Pentecostal experience, the Lovers Lane campus offers a Pentecostal experience every Sunday with persons speaking more than a dozen languages, including American Sign Language, Swahili, Kikuyu, Kimeru, French, KinyaRwanda, Portuguese, and several other Western African languages—as well as Texan English, of course.

Copeland and Gilliland share what I call some "transforming" mission and vision-driven secrets of United Methodists at Lovers Lane that we may not have previously realized are keys for the future and unity of the church. Lovers Lane continues to follow God's mission to love all people and offers a vision of being a diverse, Bible-engaging, Jesus-uplifting, challenging-in-love community. The result is a church that has persons who are deaf and hard of hearing, persons of different sexual orientations, persons who have spent ten or more years in prison, persons who are differently-abled, and persons from more than ten countries. They have persons who have come to this country as refugees, persons from strong and vibrant African United Methodist Conferences, and persons who just want a place where they don't have to fake it and are loved for who they are as beloved children of God. The testimony to God's transforming love at Lovers Lane is powerful.

The diversity at Lovers Lane brings the United Methodist stories from many life experiences and contexts into God's own story. God's story becomes concrete and clearer as persons from different walks of life encounter one another together. God speaks profoundly through everyone's story, causing us all to live in sacred tension with our own stories. These stories invite us to deepen our understanding of the mission of "making disciples of Jesus Christ for the transformation of the world." At the intersection of our conflicting stories is where heaven becomes a reality and God embraces us through grace and love.

Forward

I echo the possibility for unity and being a stronger witness together that Copeland and Gilliland encourage us to see in the One Church Plan put forward by the Council of Bishops. The Plan is not perfect, but it is hopeful and provides a way for us to be faithful to Jesus Christ in our local mission fields and in the context of our congregations, as we live and minister together as people called United Methodists.

Together offers a tangible example for good-hearted people with a deep conscience and sincere love for Jesus who continue to ask the question, "But how will the One Church Plan work?" That answer is offered in this book. I pray for all who read *Together* that God can move the individual reader and our global, diverse United Methodist family to see the possibilities.

Rev. Kalaba Chali is a United Methodist clergy member of the Great Plains Conference and currently serves as the Mercy and Justice Coordinator for the Great Plains Conference. A graduate of Africa University in Mutare, Zimbabwe, and Perkins School of Theology, Southern Methodist University in Dallas, Texas, Chali has been formed by our strong United Methodist institutions of higher education. Before serving in the Great Plains Conference, Chali served at Fern Valley UMC in Mutare, Zimbabwe; Lovers Lane UMC in Dallas, Texas; Zion UMC in Mapaville, Missouri; and First UMC in St. Charles, Missouri.

Together

INTRODUCTION

By: Stan Copeland

"Where are we going?" It's a question you've likely asked yourself while watching political turmoil on the evening news, driving on a road trip when the GPS loses its signal, or reading blogs about divisions in The United Methodist Church. Having a vision—knowing where you are going—is critical for success on road trips and in organizations, but where does the guiding vision come from?

For fifty years, United Methodists have been wandering in the wilderness searching for what it really means to be a "united" United Methodist Church. Our trend for eighty years has been bringing our Wesleyan band together, first by uniting the Protestant Methodist Church, the Methodist Episcopal Church, and the Methodist Episcopal Church, South in 1939. Unfortunately, to do so, a Central Conference system was put in place that segregated the new denomination along racial lines.

In 1968 in Dallas, the last big quest for unity came when the Evangelical United Brethren Church (EUB) came together with the Methodist Church to form The United Methodist Church. This uniting was made more complete with the EUB's insistence on the abolishment of the Central Conference and its racial segregation.

This question of "united or not united" is especially important for churches where pastors and congregants can feel as though God is calling them to very different things. How do different people with different beliefs and different goals and maybe even different dreams unify around one vision for "where we are going"?

Church Lessons

One of the early lessons I learned about The United Methodist Church that brought me to saving faith in my Lord Jesus is that local churches can be very different yet faithful at the same time. I was sixteen years old when I "surrendered to preach" (as we used to say in the country) and was invited to help an older United Methodist pastor serving a two-point charge. "Help" was defined as preaching at one of the churches so that he would not have to preach at both points on the charge every Sunday. The pastor was not in great health, but I think, in hindsight, it was more of a gracious act on his part to give a teenager heading to college and eventually seminary some pulpit experience.

One church on the charge was in a little town off of a big Texas lake but on the highway. The other church was a little country church close to the lake where newcomers were relocating and some of them were daring to walk through the doors. I can only hope that they, by God's grace, got something out of my messages, but I learned at least two powerful lessons that still guide my pastoral ministry today.

The first lesson was that our churches can be "connected" as United Methodists, even though local congregations can be only a few miles apart and can be very different theologically and socio-politically. Secondly, congregations must adapt to their often-changing mission fields, and God can raise a new vision that will bring life if the mission is ultimately about "making disciples of Jesus Christ for the transformation of the world." And maybe a third lesson: United Methodists can be the most spirit-filled, grace-motivated people on the face of the earth, who would listen to a boy preacher and treat him like he was John Wesley himself. I love The United Methodist Church.

Serving My Dream Church

Today, I find myself forty years later serving the church of my dreams, where I have served as Senior Pastor for more than twenty years. My charge today is Lovers Lane United Methodist Church (or simply "Lovers Lane" as we say, though we are still proud of our United Methodist brand). This church, its people, and its staff have taught me much about unity, sometimes in the midst of tension.

I want to make this clear at the outset: Lovers Lane is FAR from a perfect church. I don't uplift our congregation in this book to brag on how we get everything right, because we don't. I will speak about the context of our ministry to show what I see as the strength that any local church can have when it comes to resolving difficult conversations at the local level. And furthermore, what should not be a secret is that it is the Holy Spirit who orchestrates the ministry movements.

We at Lovers Lane have had our own share of glory days, as well as days of pain over the years. In the midst of changing culture and context, the people of Lovers Lane have more than risen to the occasion of ministry in the twenty-first century. They have taught me about the love of Christ that can keep God's people together if they are sold out to mission and driven by vision that causes them to dare to dream together.

In our connection as United Methodists, all of our churches have unique stories. All of our church stories are contextual and often full of both pain and joy, despair and hope, challenges and exciting movements of God's Spirit. We United Methodists have a connectional polity and discipline, a rich history with a strong theological foundation that is full of testimony to God's amazing, multi-faceted grace. We are also a people called to scriptural holiness, following the teaching of a man named Wesley. He taught us to be people of vision, a vision of holiness, that we be perfected in love and tolerant in spirit. He espoused being united in the essentials of our faith and, in the non-essentials, being accepting and tolerant of those who held different beliefs.

Lovers Lane is fast approaching its seventy-fifth anniversary, and I am the fourth full-time pastor appointed to this charge. The first pastor, Dr. Thomas Joel Shipp, served the church for thirty-one years. Tom's story is one of an orphan boy who became the legendary pastor of this great congregation, and in this book we will share a bit of his story because it is part of the local contextual history that has influenced our vision today. It is a story of how he set out to develop a church in the style of Zacchaeus, boldly following God's call to be "up a tree and out on a limb" for Jesus.

The first people who left Lovers Lane over conflict to go elsewhere were offended that Tom would allow alcoholics to be members of the church in 1945. His response to the naysayers was, "These people need us and if we are not here for people who need us, then why are we here?" By the mid-1960s Lovers Lane was the fourth largest Methodist church in the connection and said to have over three hundred families with persons in recovery of alcohol addiction at that time.

Others left the church in 1961, in the height of tensions surrounding civil rights, when Tom received into membership an African-American woman whom he had led to Christ through praying with her while visiting her in the hospital. Twenty families left the church in response to that act of racial inclusion, but by the end of the year, 587 people had joined the church. Lovers Lane became known as a church where ALL were welcomed into relationship with Jesus Christ and the community of his Church.

People come and go today to this place—the most diverse-in-every-way congregation of which I have ever been part—based on whether we align with their faith preferences and practices. Some have left through the years to move to the suburbs ("white flight"). Some have left as the church became more multicultural and colorful and too "different." Some left because they were uncomfortable with our acceptance of lesbian, gay, bisexual, transgender, or queer (LGBTQ) persons. Some apologetically said, "We are looking for a more 'neighborhood'-type church" (whatever that means). Some probably left because they couldn't understand the preacher's East Texas accent and wondered if my neck was as red as they assumed it was. But many come because Lovers Lane is unique, authentic, and some might say a bit "different" (meaning a bit "weird," yet in an attractive sort of way). And no question, it is joy-filled.

Vision-Driven

On October 20th, 1946, at the dedication of its first building, the seeds of vision for the congregation that I serve came out of a then twenty-six-year-old Tom Shipp's mouth, and more importantly, his heart. In a day when churches felt no need for mission or vision statements, nor the values that would drive the congregation, Pastor Tom Shipp said this:

> *Let's make a church and institution that stands as we say 'four-square', for what is right, what is just, what is fair, what is of good report; An institution in which there are no shams, no make-believe, no halfway measures; where thoroughness and straight-forwardness are taught and practiced. May those within this Church have high integrity, be faithful to ideals, dependable, true friends of others and loyal to Jesus.*

Today, Lovers Lane has a staff that is as diverse theologically, socio-politically, and multiculturally as our congregation. And I am happy to report that I have never worked on a staff with more unity and love.

Introduction

This is a product of our congregation's spirit and underscores our health and commitment to mission and vision.

On our staff, among our diversity of young and old, female and male, able-bodied and differently-abled, we have had five African pastors under appointment in the last decade: a Zambian, two Zimbabweans, a Congolese, and a Kenyan from the Kenyan Methodist Church. We also have had ten persons go to seminary in the past five years and all of those but three—who are gay and lesbian Christians—are in process of ordination.

Our staff and lay leadership, not all of whom share common beliefs on matters related to homosexuality, share a common love, respect, and spirit of cooperation with each other. In other words, they share a commitment to do ministry together. All embrace our congregation's unity and hope for more contextual flexibility in our denomination going forward. All of our staff support the One Church Plan[2], which allows local churches and pastors to assess their mission fields and make local decisions where decisions are necessary.

A Book of Hope

Together was inspired by the Uniting Methodists[3] vision and values (www.unitingmethodists.com/vision) along the topic of "Fixed and

---

[2] This is the plan the Council of Bishops of our United Methodist Church have voted as their preference out of the work of The Commission on a Way Forward.
[3] "Uniting Methodists" is a movement within the denomination working to support the One Church Plan and its vision for our global church.

Free." The vision is rich in biblical foundation and straightforward in support of the One Church Plan.

This book will share the belief and perspective of this "fifty-nine-and-holding" pastor and is co-authored by Rev. Scott Gilliland, who came to our staff in 2010 as a twenty-two-year-old Children's Ministry Assistant. Scott was just ordained an elder, as was his gifted wife, Raegan, at the 2018 North Texas Annual Conference. Scott is hopelessly, or shall I say *hopefully* marked as a Millennial. He is also one of the finest young preachers I have ever worked with.

My guess is that every generation of United Methodist pastors has looked at the crop of preachers in the new generation coming up and has been woefully skeptical about the future of the church. I remember my Silent Generation mentor, Dr. William H. Hinson, the Senior Pastor of First United Methodist Church Houston 1982-2001 and one of the founders of the Confessing Movement in 1995. When I was serving under his leadership, he reminded me, in somewhat of a going-to-hell-in-a-handbasket sort of way, that my generation had never seen The United Methodist Church in anything but decline. Since we have been declining for the past fifty years, the reality is stark. He was right, of course, and his observation, said with a degree of grief, still held hope that things could one day soon be different. The bigger question is, "Will our generation (Boomers) be remembered for splintering the denomination again?"

Introduction

Like many in my generation, I have been guilty of being judgmental and questioning Millennials like Scott on everything from their work habits, to their professional attire (or lack thereof), their cocky assuredness of knowing everything, and their carefree attitude about the future. I see our millennial colleagues, however, and I am very hopeful for the church. Scott and his Lovers Lane colleagues seem to really "get" the culture they are part of and are trying to reach for Christ. They speak the language, technologically and otherwise, and see the mess of division my generation largely is leaving them with as the "state of the church." We need to listen to Scott and the vast majority of others of his generation who are by and large pleading with us to change.

Far from despair, these young pastors and leaders still have hope, spiritual grounding, and a Millennial brand of confidence that they, with God's help, can fix this myopic, lack-of-vision mess of division that we are passing on.

The larger church today, and especially the people called United Methodists, suffers from vision and dream anemia. The visionless state of our existence has us on the brink of what could potentially be a church split over theology and social agenda, pulling so-called "progressives" and "traditionalists" apart. Just as slavery became the divisive matter leading to a separation in 1844, today it's how we view those who are LGBTQ.

The divisive views have to do with what the Bible says and doesn't say: about whether people can love and marry the one they love no matter their sexual orientation, and about matters of calling and ordination regarding people who must not be reduced to the consonants of LGBTQ. Though not a United Methodist, but certainly admired by many of us for his prophetic voice, William Sloane Coffin said,

> *"It is not Scripture that creates hostility to homosexuality, but rather hostility to homosexuals that prompts some Christians to recite a few sentences from Paul and retain passages from an otherwise discarded Old Testament law code. In abolishing slavery and in ordaining women we've gone beyond biblical literalism. It's time we did the same with gays and lesbians. The problem is not how to reconcile homosexuality with scriptural passages that condemn it, but rather how to reconcile the rejection and punishment of homosexuals with the love of Christ. It can't be done."*[4]

The sooner we get to this realization and admission, the sooner we engage in life-giving Wesleyan ways that God has blessed our people with for nearly 235 years.

A United Methodist Vision?

The lifeblood of the church must be our vision. The driving hope is that the vision of The United Methodist Church will become clearer and even more compelling for Christ's sake. It is my hope that this book can, in an indirect way, be a voice for Methodists who wish to

---

[4] Coffin, W. S. (2004). *Credo*. Westminster John Knox Press, 158

remain united. A vision is, succinctly stated, a church's preferred future—its holy pursuit.

If we want to stay a United Methodist people, we must develop a vision of what life together looks like, knowing that we find ourselves perhaps in temples or tabernacles, but always centered around the unifying sacrament of the Lord's Table. This book is ultimately about raising a vision of "uniting" that is more than just "staying together," and it encourages shifting our talk and action throughout the world to be focused on our mission. At Lovers Lane, this is our stated and clarifying vision of who we are and where we are going:

> *To be one dynamic community, passionately engaging the Bible, uplifting Jesus in worship and loving service, and challenging in love that which divides.*

I believe this is a significant omission in our larger denomination: **We have no stated shared vision as United Methodists.** And when we prayerfully consider what it would be like to have a compelling vision of our future together, I daresay that God would not say, "Separate, that's the best way forward and, in the end, it is the easiest way." My experience of God is that God's leadership is always the path of greatest challenge that requires ultimate dependence on the Holy Spirit to lead, guide, and direct toward the ways of Jesus.

At Lovers Lane, our stated vision also propels us into a stated dream.[5] A dream is a big, holy, audacious goal that no one can possibly achieve without supernatural involvement. A God-sized dream is so big that people laugh, or at least smile, when they first hear it. I believe we have dreamers, millions of them even, throughout our global denomination, but until we have a stated vision, I fear those dreams will remain unclear and unachievable. Vision truly is the key.

Unity Hunger

The hunger for unity has today gone from a growl to a roar in our country. Whether the church still has a voice that will be heard is unfortunately in question. The jury is still out on whether United Methodists value being "united" over other values that some see as big enough and essential enough to merit a denominational divorce. My daily prayer is that God will raise us up to not only share a vision together of the future but will free our local congregations to dream about what God wants them to be about.

I believe that United Methodists can *Together* be a templing and tabernacling[6] church spreading the Table of our Lord as wide as God's love reaches. It is also a heartfelt prayer that every member of the body of Christ know that each local expression of the body—local churches and congregations of all sizes, in towns and cities, villages and

---

[5] The Lovers Lane Dream Statement can be found in the Appendix at the end of the book.

[6] More on these funny sounding terms in Chapter 1.

neighborhoods—be reminded that our mission fields may be different and our chosen approaches may be varied, but we can trust a connection that allows us to uplift our Wesleyan heritage and theology, and we can be all that God ever intended for us to be for our Lord Jesus Christ's sake.

Let us also be forever reminded that Scripture is primarily a witness to Jesus Christ—the Author and Perfecter of our faith. It is His Table, and at this Table ALL the people of the world are welcome. May God keep us together and empower us as people of the temple, tabernacle, and the Lord's Table to transform the divided, separated, arrogant-spirited world. Scott and I humbly present our hearts and our hope against hope for a United Methodist Church moving forward together.

Stan Copeland,
Senior Pastor of Lovers Lane United Methodist Church
April 1, (April Fools' Day) 1998 to Present

Together

PREFACE

By: Scott Gilliland, *adapted from a blog posted Nov. 2017*

In November of 2017, the local church I serve, Lovers Lane United Methodist Church, hosted a gathering of area clergy and lay leaders interested in learning more about a movement called "Uniting Methodists." Leading the presentation and ensuing discussion were the Rev. Rachel Baughman of Oak Lawn UMC in Dallas and the Rev. Dr. Stan Copeland of Lovers Lane UMC.

I respect both of these leaders immensely, not only as colleagues, but for their personal impact on my life and faith. Rachel was actually the Director of Children's Ministries when I was in the sixth grade at W.C. Martin UMC in Bedford, Texas. Stan has been my boss and mentor for the better part of the last decade. That respect for the two leaders was shared by the room, and it was seeing them together on stage that likely sparked more than a little curiosity amongst those who came.

On the left (literally and figuratively), sat a young, progressive woman with clerical collar, black plastic glasses, and dreads pulled neatly into a bun. On the right was an *ahem* experienced, traditionalist man with suit and sweater-vest, a haircut that hasn't changed in thirty-five years, and an East Texas accent that hasn't changed for far longer. (Stan would like to point out that I obviously have hair jealousy. I won't deny it.) Sitting together, they perhaps sum up Uniting Methodists in one image.

The two of them shared from the heart, both speaking of their great love for The United Methodist Church and the ways in which it has shaped them in their personal and professional lives. Rachel spoke of being a sixth-generation Methodist pastor and the tension she now felt between living into both the unity and justice we are called to in Scripture. Rachel serves a church that is a Reconciling Congregation with 70 percent of her members somewhere on the LGBTQ spectrum and located in the heart of the neighborhood for that community.

Stan spoke of his journey from learning the ropes at First United Methodist Church in Houston, Texas, as an associate under Dr. William H. Hinson, the then flag-bearer for evangelical Methodists who first called for "amicable separation" at the 2004 General Conference. Lovers Lane is a church that has been strengthened by what Stan calls "Wesleyan evangelicalism," epitomized in the mission of "Loving ALL people into relationship with Jesus Christ." Both Rachel and Stan spoke with heartfelt hope for a future that allows the two of them to remain in connectional covenant.

We watched the now-famous "sugar packet" video[7] explaining the four basic categories of United Methodists on the subject of full inclusion of LGBTQ persons:

---

[7] To see this video, go to unitingmethodists.com/resources/ and watch the video titled "Introductory Conversation on the Uniting Methodist Movement." Tom Berlin's "Sugar Packet" presentation starts at 9:37 on the video.

Progressive Non-Compatibilists—those who will not accept anything but full inclusion throughout the global denomination.

Traditionalist Non-Compatibilists—those who will not accept any changes that move toward more progressive positions in the Book of Discipline.

Progressive and Traditionalist Compatibilists—those who hold differing views on inclusion, but are willing to remain in covenant with the "other side" and hope the denomination will find a way to stay united.

At the gathering, participants shared discussion over table talks about why we are United Methodists, what we believe is the greatest strength of our denomination, and why or why not we believe the denomination should seek to stay together. I found the day spiritually, emotionally, and intellectually moving, and I'm excited to see the movement progress.

The Uniting Methodists are attempting to accomplish two things: 1) Address the very real and present issues surrounding full inclusion of LGBTQ people in The United Methodist Church, and 2) Establish a new culture and framework for understanding ourselves as a denomination with pluralistic tendencies.

To the second point, I see this expressed in the Uniting Methodists' vision and mission statements, especially the intriguing "Fixed and Free" statements. Jesus Christ, the Holy Spirit, the Church, and Unity are all described as "Fixed and Free"—borrowing the image of the tabernacle and the temple in the Old Testament—and something inside me immediately identifies with their naming the tensions we so often find at the core of the Christian faith.

It is my view that the hermeneutics (the branch of knowledge that deals with interpretation of Bible or literary texts) surrounding homosexuality in the Bible have been researched/discussed/written about/preached to death. We've parsed, we've contextualized, we've cherry-picked, and we've gotten nowhere. It's one of the reasons we all wait with bated breath for the work of the Commission on a Way Forward to save us from ourselves at the called General Conference in 2019. Today, I'm wondering if we're discussing the right thing.

A Church Divided

Paul's letter to the church in Rome is frequently cited in the inclusion debate, specifically his litany of "sins of the flesh" found in chapter one, where a word or phrase appears that may or may not reference homosexuality, depending on which United Methodist you ask.

I find it interesting that Romans is lifted up so often in this discussion, because I actually do believe the letter could be prescriptive for us as a church not unlike the one Paul wrote to in Rome. Deeply divided. Progressive Gentiles versus Traditionalist Jews. A struggle to find vision, direction, and leadership. Stuck.

Sound familiar?

For the first thirteen chapters of Romans, Paul takes his time developing what is widely considered to be his masterpiece of theological writing, bridging the gap between the camps of Jews and Gentiles. "Yes," he says, the Jewish tradition and the promise of Abraham and the Law as it was known are important and should be remembered and respected. "And yes," he says, Christ is available to all, and the promise has been extended, and Christ is the living Law whom we now are under. Both are true, and must be true, or else the Church would suffer as a result.

Then we get to chapter fourteen where Paul's attention shifts and he no longer preaches about lofty doctrinal issues. Instead, he brings his focus to where division has been felt most practically in the Roman church: pork. A whole chapter of one of the most important books of the Bible dedicated to whether or not a good Christian eats pork! So much for a masterpiece.

It's Not About Pork

Romans 14 is not about pork, not really. In fact, Paul also references another practical division present in the church: whether one set day should be recognized as the Sabbath or not. Do we eat pork, do we celebrate Sabbath…? What he's really talking about is this:

"What do we do when we disagree about faithful Christian practice?"

His answer is simple and straightforward:

The faith that you have, have as your own conviction before God. Blessed are those who have no reason to condemn themselves because of what they approve. But those who have doubts are condemned if they eat, because they do not act from faith; for whatever does not proceed from faith is sin. (Rom 14:22-23)

As a denomination, we've been arguing over the subject of homosexuality, but it's not about homosexuality, not really. I think at the core of this debate, and certainly debates we will encounter in the years and decades to come, what we're really arguing about is what constitutes faithful Christian practice, the same thing the church in Rome argued about two thousand years ago.

Before I'm accused of trivializing the conversation by trying to relate this to eating pork, understand that a) eating pork was a grave concern for first-century Jews and far from a trivial matter, but more importantly, b) our own Book of Discipline would suggest that this really is an argument about practice. And I quote:

*"The **practice** of homosexuality is incompatible with Christian teaching."* [8]

It seems that for many in our country and throughout our world, there is a deeply held belief that homosexual acts could not, for them, be an act of faith. And yet, for so many others in our country—and yes,

---

[8] Book of Discipline 2016, ¶ 304.3

around the world—monogamous, covenantal, same-sex relationships are seen to be faithful and good. I would suggest that Paul has already spoken to this precise issue, the issue of division, not in the use of one word that may or may not mean what we want it to mean, but in a whole chapter of his most celebrated text. A chapter that is devoted to a theology of church.

What we have in the UMC is a faith issue, and it has nothing to do with homosexuality. We don't have faith in each other. We've lost trust along the way. As Paul says, if we truly have faith that our brothers and sisters in our pews and churches around the world are walking faithfully with God, then ***"Who are you to pass judgment on servants of another?"*** (Rom 14:4) Paul is calling on us to release our grip just a bit and allow there to be dynamism in the way we live out our faith, person to person, community to community, church to church.

A Romans 14 Church

The Uniting Methodists, to me, represent a Romans 14 church: A church that defines clearly the essential doctrines upon which our faith is built, and a church that encourages trust in the individual's relationship with God, open to where that might lead us in practice.

There will be some who cannot envision a church like this, or believe fervently that progressive and traditionalist views on LGBTQ inclusion are simply incompatible, but for those of us somewhere in the middle, rooted in our beliefs and yet committed to remaining in relationship with one another, I believe Romans 14 offers us hope.

Arguing is easy. Building trust is hard. Maybe that's why arguing has been our default for so long now, at least at General Conference. The honest truth is, I don't think most local churches are still fighting about these topics, but then again, there's far greater trust in most local churches than there is at General Conference. I look forward to future conversations with colleagues and congregants surrounding the future of our denomination we all love.

Rooted in Scripture

There is one body and one Spirit, just as you were called to the one hope of your calling, one Lord, one faith, one baptism, one God and Father of all, who is above all and through all and in all. (Eph 4:4-6)

Rooted in Wesley

[Schism] is evil in itself. To separate ourselves from a body of living Christians, with whom we were before united, is a grievous breach of the law of love. It is the nature of love to unite us together; and the greater the love, the stricter the union. And while this continues in its strength, nothing can divide those whom love has united. It is only when our love grows cold, that we can think of separating from our brethren. And this is certainly the case with any who willingly separate from their Christian brethren. The pretenses for separation may be innumerable, but want of love is always the real cause; otherwise they would still hold the unity of the Spirit in the bound of peace.
(John Wesley, "On Schism," Sermon 75)

CHAPTER ONE

Temple, Tabernacle, and Uncle Doug's Guitar

By: Scott Gilliland

In ancient Israel, many leaders believed that holiness was established by returning to God and keeping God's instructions. For Israel, God's laws and commandments were fixed and reliable, but the people strayed and needed to turn around to get right with God. This theology is located in the Temple, the fixed place where God resides, to which faithful people could return.

Other leaders in ancient Israel perceived that holiness was found by following God wherever God led them. God's presence was perceived as mobile and free, leading God's people on a journey, through particular contexts and into whatever new experiences God had for them. This theology is symbolized by the Tabernacle, which was the visible reminder that God led the Israelites away from slavery into freedom and a new promise to fulfill.

Both theological perspectives were deeply embedded in the collective conscience of the Israelite people. These seemingly irreconcilable positions contributed in part to the split between the Southern Kingdom—who believed in a God who was fixed—and the Northern Kingdom—who believed in a God who was free. Both perspectives are biblical and evident in the church today, and both are necessary.[9]

* * *

This year, I spent the post-Christmas week with my mom's side of the extended family in Mississippi. We used to get together more often, at least twice a year, but as the cousins got older and got married, and families started growing, it has become more difficult to get everyone

---

[9] "Fixed and Free," UnitingMethodists.com/vision

together. So to find a whole week where almost everyone could be in one spot was a joy.

One evening, my uncle Doug and I were chatting. He was telling me about an especially meaningful gift he had received. See, Uncle Doug is planning to retire in the next few years, and he has always wanted to learn how to play guitar. It just so happens one of his friends likes to make custom-built guitars for friends as a hobby. So, for Christmas, Uncle Doug got a powder-blue electric guitar with little red dice as the tone and volume knobs.

I asked him how it was going, trying to learn how to play guitar after all these years of saying, "One day . . ." The hardest part surprised him, he said. It wasn't learning scales. It wasn't contorting his hand to play chords. What surprised him was how much his fingers hurt pressing down the strings.

If you've ever learned how to play guitar, you know what he means. The way guitars work is there are six strings fixed on something called a bridge, a fixed place on the body of the guitar. From there, the strings are stretched across the length of the body and neck and then wrapped around tuning pegs. You twist and turn these freely moving pegs to get the perfect pitch from each string. One side fixed, one side free, and in the middle, on the frets, you press down on the strings with your fingertips. Which isn't easy.

Temple, Tabernacle, and Uncle Doug's Guitar

Our fingertips are sensitive, perfectly designed to warn our bodies when something is hot or sharp. But when learning to play guitar you must press into thin, metal strings held under incredibly high tension, and it hurts.

Because tension can be painful.

When we talk about tension, we usually talk about it in a negative way. When you walk into a room and "could cut the tension with a knife," it's not a good thing. And when learning to play guitar, tension is painful, but it's also where the music happens.

And if you've ever heard a master guitarist, you know that when you learn how to play in the tension, you can make beautiful music.

I think The United Methodist Church is like a guitar, tension abounding between the "fixed" and "free" camps of traditionalists and progressivists, and many of us are caught in the middle. The response to this tension, for some, is to suggest a schism or split in our denomination. Like taking wire cutters to the strings of a guitar, with one cut you could eliminate the most immediate tension as the strings spring back to their respective sides. No more tension. No more pain. And no more music.

So I think that the tension might actually be good. I think that sometimes we look at the Christian faith and we see things that might look like they're in tension. And maybe you're outside the Christian faith and you think those things are contradictory. We say that God is eternal, and yet God is also in the person of Jesus Christ. I mean, how in the world is that possible? However, I don't think that tensions are contradictory in the Christian faith; I believe they are complementary. And that's the question we have to wrestle with first: Are the tensions we find in The United Methodist Church contradictory or complementary?

Contradictory tensions are those you need to cut, those you need to allow to go separate ways, because they just don't fit together. But if the tensions complement one another, like the two ends of a guitar, and music can be made in the middle, then that's a beautiful opportunity that we don't want to waste.

Tabernacle and Temple

To help understand the value of remaining both "fixed" and "free" in our theology, we can turn our attention to Scripture, specifically the stories of the tabernacle in Exodus 25 and the temple in 1 Kings 6. Both texts describe God commanding the Israelites to construct a building—one while they are wandering in the wilderness, the other while they are establishing a nation. In some ways, these are very different buildings, in some ways they are very similar, and it's these similarities and differences that can guide us in our own tensions.

In Exodus, after Moses and the Israelites flee captivity in Egypt, they wander in the wilderness for what will become forty years, searching for the promised land to call home. Early in their journey, God says to Moses:

Tell the Israelites to take for me an offering; from all whose hearts prompt them to give you shall receive the offering for me. This is the offering that you shall receive from them: gold, silver, and bronze, blue, purple, and crimson yarns and fine linen, goats' hair, tanned rams' skins, fine leather, acacia wood, oil for the lamps, spices for the anointing oil and for the fragrant incense, onyx stones and gems to be set in the ephod and for the breast piece. And have them make me a sanctuary, so that I may dwell among them. In accordance with all that I show you concerning the pattern of the tabernacle and of all its furniture, so you shall make it. (Exod 25:2-9)

God is describing in vivid detail a tabernacle, or sacred tent, that will serve as a space of holy worship and reverence while the Israelites wander the wilderness without a home to call their own. With no firm place to settle, the Israelites in this part of their story need God to move with them and offer a home of sorts in their homelessness.

When we arrive at 1 Kings 6, the Israelites are in a very different place, literally and figuratively. They have settled in the promised land and have now turned their attention to establishing themselves as a powerful people in a hotly contested region of the world. Where earlier they needed a sense of home and belonging in a strange land, they now need stability and security in who God is establishing them to be as a nation.

Now the word of the LORD came to Solomon, "Concerning this house that you are building, if you will walk in my statutes, obey my ordinances, and keep all my commandments by walking in them, then I will establish my promise with you, which I made to your father David. I will dwell among the children of Israel, and will not forsake my people Israel." So Solomon built the house, and finished it. (1 Kgs 6:11-14)

Notice something about these two buildings and how God describes them. The details change—the tabernacle is cloth and nomadic, the temple is stone and unmoving—but one thing remains constant in both. One thing is worth God repeating in the instructive verses. Make this tabernacle, God says in Exodus, "so that I may dwell among them." Build this temple, God says in 1 Kings, and "I will dwell among the children of Israel."

To dwell.

This is the constant we ought not miss. Beyond the cloth and the stone and the gems and the rams' horns and the statutes and the ordinances, God dwelling with God's children, this is the purpose of both the tabernacle and the temple. Whether God's Spirit is where it has always been or whether God's Spirit is on the move, God is always dwelling with God's children.

Now, this sounds nice perhaps, but it certainly sounds like tension as well. How can God be fixed and free at the same time? Isn't this contradictory?

And honestly, doesn't one of these options just sound better anyway? Wouldn't it be better if God was just a constant truth built in stone, or if God was just a wild, freely moving God in the wilderness? I imagine many of us resonate with one image or the other a little more. We gravitate more to the idea of a temple or a tabernacle just a bit.

So let's stop for a moment and consider what faith in a God who is only in the temple or a God who is only in the tabernacle would look like.

God of the Tabernacle

The tabernacle is God at God's most free.

Free to move with God's people.
Free to call anywhere "home."
Free to be wherever God's people are.

It reminds me of when Jesus says that God is like a shepherd in search of one lost sheep. In Matthew and Luke, Jesus compares people to sheep, and asks the potent question:

> *What do you think? If a shepherd has a hundred sheep, and one of them has gone astray, does he not leave the ninety-*

nine on the mountains and go in search of the one that went astray? (Matt 18:12,)

What a compelling image of God this proves to be! All of us have at times felt like the one lost sheep, and we need to believe that God is relentlessly pursuing each and every one of us at all times. Can't you remember those moments when you felt God meet you in the lost places of your life with love and mercy and grace when you needed them most?

A wandering, searching, free God is a good thing.

And for many of us, this is the image of God we gravitate toward most. We find a free God compelling and we find ourselves on the free end of debates in the church, but I think a God who is only free has very real limits.

I have a toddler named Andie Jane, and she loves potato chips, or as she calls them, "bips." When she gets hungry for a snack, she'll walk up to me, tug on my pant leg, look up with her big blue eyes, and say, "Dada . . . bips peez!" ("Please" is a hard word too.)

If I tell her no, she wastes no time running down the hall, finding Raegan (my wife), and asking her, "Mama . . . bips peez!" in the hopes that she'll get a better answer. If you've raised children, you've no doubt experienced something similar time and time again.

I wonder, how often do we treat God the same way that Andie treats her parents? By this I mean, how often do we receive an answer from God that we are not satisfied with, and so we spend time in "prayer" or reinterpretation of Scripture until—wouldn't you know it?!—God comes around to our way of thinking! I find that in a culture of confirmation bias (the idea that most everyone is biased toward reinforcing their preconceived beliefs) we can abuse our relationship with God to the point that God is reduced to our personal cheerleader who wholly supports whatever thoughts and beliefs come across our hearts and minds. Put simply: If we desire only a free God, we run the risk of essentially following our own wills.

Lord knows I've been guilty of conforming God to my image too often in my own life, and one of the great gifts in the Christian faith is its ability to challenge us with a gospel that will invariably ask us to reevaluate what we think we know.

God of the Temple

The temple is God at God's most fixed—not stuck in the mud, but eternally true! The fixed temple is the same yesterday, today, and forever.

Fixed in stone as the sacred place for a priestly nation.
Fixed as the place Israel can finally call "home."
Fixed as an anchor where God could always be found.

I was privileged to travel to the Holy Land while I was a student at Perkins School of Theology, and it was there that I got to see the stones that form the Western Wall of the temple mount, the foundation upon which the temple of Jewish tradition had historically stood. I watched as throngs of women and men—mostly Jews, but some Christians as well—gathered at the wall in prayer, some so close they even kissed the stones as they wedged prayerfully scribbled pieces of paper into the cracks.

I was struck by how meaningful a place, even stones themselves, truly can be for those in need of a proverbial "rock" in their life. It reminds me of another image Jesus gives us for God, this time as the father of a prodigal son. You likely know the story found in Luke 15 of a young man who demands an early inheritance only to squander it on a careless lifestyle, eventually finding himself penniless, working as a lowly swineherd, and eating the slop meant for the pigs. When he remembers his father's love and mercy, he knows where to go: home. As he approaches the family estate, while he is still far off from the gate, his father runs out like a fool, spurred on by a reckless love that greets his son. The father's mercy and love are proved to be rock solid.

All of us have had moments in life when we needed something rock solid to rely on in our faith. Not unlike the prodigal son returning home, we know that we can find our God through timeless Scripture, eternal truths, and yes, sacred spaces. What a gift these are in the Christian faith. For many of us, it is why a fixed God resonates with us most, and we find ourselves on the fixed end of debates in the church as well.

And yet, if I think about the Parable of the Prodigal Son, I must also remember the son's older brother, who stayed within the father's boundaries. You might even say he lived by the "ordinances and commandments" mentioned in the temple text of 1 Kings, but he is grieved by his father's ability to extend grace to someone he thought beyond it. Why such judgment from the older brother? Why such a hardness of heart? It seems he saw his younger brother, "this son of yours" as he calls him, as irredeemably sinful and believed he should be excluded from his father's table.

My question is this: If we desire only a fixed God, like a hard-hearted brother intent on including only those who meet our standards, will the Table ever be small enough?

If the "ordinances and commandments" mentioned in 1 Kings become our defining aspects, will anyone really ever measure up? Do you or I measure up? I know I don't, and yet how easy is it for us to whip out the measuring sticks with a "you must be THIS holy to ride the ride" approach to life in the church.

If we truly want a smaller table, I worry we'll never be satisfied until we find ourselves sitting at a TV tray . . . a table for one.

Seeing God as Fixed *and* Free

Who are we as United Methodists? Do we worship a God of the tabernacle or a God of the temple? Which is it? Doesn't it feel like we're in a season where the loudest voices on each end of our contemporary debates are demanding we pick?

Here's a novel idea: Why not both?

Why can't we be a denomination—I would even say why can't we *continue* to be a denomination—that uplifts the God of tabernacle and temple? A God who is both fixed and free?

We're so close. We're so close to snipping the strings, cutting the tension, because "it's too painful" and "we just can't do this anymore." And some of us would choose a free path. And some of us would choose a fixed path. And in the middle would be no tension, no pain . . . and no music.

Is that the kind of faith that we want? Is that a gospel that the world needs to hear? Is that a gospel that will transform the world in which we live?

Or . . .

Can we claim a Gospel that uplifts both a God who is free and a God who is fixed?

Can we proclaim a Gospel that says "God knows where to find me" and "I know where to find God"?

Can we worship a God so sold out to love, grace, and redemption that God will scour the ends and depths of the earth and will also stay exactly where God's been so we know where to find God?

Is that not a God and a Gospel worth serving?

Is that not a God worth living in some tension for?

We're making music, friends. Maybe we aren't playing well at General Conference, but in our local churches, where we hold each other in tension out of love for each other and for Christ, we're making music. Yet we're about ready to quit.

As United Methodists, can we uplift an identity that boldly proclaims those essential anchoring truths in our faith, while also listening intently for the Spirit's movements in our mission fields? Can we trust in our sisters and brothers to live in the tension with us and know that sometimes we're simply going to disagree, yet God is still here?

I believe United Methodists have a unique opportunity right now to speak loudly and clearly that divisions taking root in our culture and in our country will be uprooted in our church, and that we will find a way forward where everyone can follow the God of the tabernacle and temple together. While we may disagree, we can be united in the Good News of a Savior named Jesus Christ who we proclaim to a world in desperate need of redemption in every place where God's temples may be found and where God's tabernacles can go.

Temple, Tabernacle, and Uncle Doug's Guitar

Together

CHAPTER TWO

Jesus, Spare Us from the Ukuleles

By: Stan Copeland

Jesus was the fixed, constant Word who became flesh and tabernacled among us (*John 1:14*). *He was born in the royal lineage centered on the Temple, as the God who is fixed. He also offers good news to ever-expanding circles of people, beyond boundaries and borders, as the God who is also free.*

He reveals a higher way, a holistic vision of the kingdom. God's love in Christ calls us to a life in which we learn to place our love toward God and others above any partisan position or doctrine, no matter how well-informed we might be. All of us, without exception, can be guilty of wanting to be right more than in love with each other.

We bear witness to the holistic way of Jesus, which calls us both to return to our Wesleyan tradition and to follow into the new spaces where Christ will lead us. We seek to keep our hearts and minds centered on Jesus, so we are open to wherever the catholic spirit of God's love might lead us. Amid complexity, we trust a God who is fixed in covenant relationship and free to extend that covenant life to all, a Triune God whose grace saves us, sanctifies us, and moves us toward perfection.[10]

* * *

The Judeo-Christian tradition has struggled with unity for thousands of years and the church from the beginning has dealt with schism. The mainline of our denomination has experienced splintering over our 230+ years.

---

[10] "Jesus: Fixed and Free," UnitingMethodists.com/vision

17

2018 will be a year of ongoing debate in our United Methodist Church as we seek a way forward through controversial matters that have been under debate for the better part of fifty years. The main source of the debate focuses on matters related to sexuality, namely "compatibility with Christian teaching," sanctity of marriage, and the rite of ordination.

Let me say that as pastor of Lovers Lane for twenty years, I know that theologically this church I serve is very eclectic—the temple and the tabernacle people are together here—and I imagine many pastors and laity alike could so testify about the churches that they serve. Socio-politically we are very diverse too. As a pastor, I don't always enjoy talking about matters that are divisive, as most of us are not naturally "activists," but also, I believe most of us are striving for authentic ways to be accepting of all people to whom we present the gospel of our Lord.

At Lovers Lane, we choose not to "break covenant" or take action that is against the Book of Discipline, but we do hear sincerely and poignantly those who say that our denomination's words are hurtful.

Four Ukuleles

Scott related the tension to a guitar and the pain of playing a guitar's steel strings as a beginner. I was a beginning guitar player twenty years before Scott was born. He said it is in the tension of the strings where beautiful music comes, and he is right. But when he used that metaphor as a sermon illustration in worship, he used a ukulele to illustrate a point about the guitar because it was easier to handle and still bring forth his illustration. Everyone knows that a ukulele does not have steel strings and can be played without pain, even with the tension fully intact.

However, I daresay that only so much ukulele music can be endured at one time. When I think of the ukulele, I think of Tiny Tim singing "Tiptoe Through the Tulips" in the 1970s. If you remember Tiny Tim and the song, you no doubt shudder as the memory comes to mind, and if you don't remember him, look the video up on YouTube and you'll be shuddering soon enough.

My concern is that The United Methodist Church, in an attempt to escape the tension, may end up choosing to divide and become like "four ukuleles." My concern, if this happens, is that we will lose our witness and diminish our mission because the world we are called to transform will not listen long to ukuleles.

The following explanation is too simplistic, but basically United Methodists are in four categories. There are those that believe the conversation around sexual ethics and LGBTQ inclusion is a matter of:

- **Justice**: Everything we have said in the past must be changed. Full inclusion of LGBTQ persons must be the global rule, and if it is not, we don't know if we want to be associated with The United Methodist Church.

- **Covenant**: What we currently say in our Book of Discipline must be upheld and obeyed by all. Furthermore, if local churches are given the option to decide on matters related to marriage and annual conferences are given the option to decide on matters of ordination, then we're out of here.

- **Unity**: We uplift the message that there is more that we have in common than our differences. Saying less is more helpful to our way forward and removing the post-1968 language on sexuality is needed. Our local churches should be able to decide on these matters, and there will be plenty of "conservative" churches and "liberal" churches under the large tent of United Methodism, just like there have been for decades.

- **Whatever**: What my local church does matters, but what another United Methodist Church does at General Conference is their business. We like what our name is and what our local and global mission work does for persons in need, but we don't care about the ineffective, divisive politics of the General Church.

Do you hear the ukulele twang?

Jesus: Templer and Tabernacler

In ancient Israel, many leaders believed that holiness was established by returning to God and keeping God's instructions. Other leaders in ancient Israel perceived that holiness was found by following God wherever God led them and sometimes that required them to do things differently.

In the Gospel of Luke we see the following scene:

> *Then Jesus, filled with the power of the Spirit, returned to Galilee, and a report about him spread through all the surrounding country. He began to teach in their synagogues and was praised by everyone.*
>
> *When he came to Nazareth, where he had been brought up, he went to the synagogue on the sabbath day, as was his custom. He stood up to read, and the scroll of the prophet Isaiah was given to him. He unrolled the scroll and found the place where it was written:*
>
> > *"The Spirit of the Lord is upon me,*
> > *because he has anointed me*
> > *to bring good news to the poor.*
> > *He has sent me to proclaim release to the captives*
> > *and recovery of sight to the blind,*
> > *to let the oppressed go free,*
> > *to proclaim the year of the Lord's favor." (Luke 4:14-19)*

Jesus was a "templer" and pushed his listeners to return to God and God's ways. When he began his ministry, he did not do so outside the established religion. He started in the synagogue, in the Jewish version of local church, precisely where a *fixed* faithful person would expect.

And if you know the rest of the story, you know he was run out of there.

I know several in my own congregation who have had this same experience as they cling to a traditional faith, but because of who they are and how they have come to understand who God made them to be, they have been outright rejected by the "temples" they used to call home.

When we read the beginning of John's Gospel, we hear Jesus described in a "tabernacle" way:

> **And the Word became flesh and lived among us, and we have seen his glory, the glory as of a father's only son, full of grace and truth.** *(John 1:14)*

Jesus was a "tabernacler." In the original Greek, the language used even describes his "living among us" as "tabernacling" with humanity. And just as Jesus in the *fixed* temple also moves freely, here we see a *free* Jesus who is also *fixed* with not only grace, but truth as well. If we want a full picture of who Jesus is, we have to take into account how Jesus is both *fixed* and *free*.

Mission Diversion

One of the things that grieves me over our divides is that it diverts us from our mission to "make disciples of Jesus Christ for the transformation of the world."

We live in a divided world with accusations running rampant and offensive words being spouted way too freely. We must not be transformed by the world into "haters" or bow at the altar of divisions that the world puts forth, with an "us versus them" mentality. We are called to make followers of Jesus and all that he is about.

The best intent is not meant to persuade you to join a "side." Nor is it meant to say that those who are of the "temple persuasion" or the "tabernacle persuasion" are right or wrong. How can we stand united going forward as we struggle with the whys and the hows of being a "United" Methodist Church?

I am committed to unity within our denomination but not for "unity's sake" or some kind of shallow unity. I am for unity that recognizes the tension in everyone NOT seeing things exactly the same. Why? Because we as a United Methodist Church have the chance to model how we don't all have to believe alike to be together and serve side-by-side. We have had very liberal churches, very conservative churches, and everything in the middle for a long time. What one of those churches does may be different than how I would do it, but in all honesty it does not really impact me, or our local church, unless it is immoral, unethical, intentionally anti-Bible, or against the grace and truth that Jesus stands for.

Herein lies the rub.

Forward Movement with Jesus

Any movement forward must uplift the unifying grace and truth of Jesus. Now, I realize that within our United Methodist churches we don't even all agree on Jesus. Every United Methodist church that I have ever served has had a "Don't Say Jesus" Sunday School class or a "Jesus Lite" group. I can even remember losing one of the leaders at Lovers Lane who was not comfortable with us saying the Apostles' Creed.

Is there enough to keep us together in our mutually held beliefs about Jesus, our Doctrinal Standards, and our mission to make disciples of Jesus? It is my testimony that Jesus is my Savior and has redeemed me through his life, death, resurrection, and ascension. In this way he proves his full divinity.

At the same time, Jesus is my Lord in that he knows our human life experience because he came down to live life on earth and therefore experienced what we do: joy, wonderment, pain, agony, and even death. In being fully human we can follow him to teach us to love God and others. I trust Jesus, who is fixed in covenant relationship and free to extend that covenant life to all. He is one of the persons of the Triune God whose grace saves.

Cultural Influences

Too often today the church finds itself bowing at another altar, the one of so-called political correctness. We don't want to offend anyone by bringing up Jesus or inviting others to come to faith in him. Dr. Billy Abraham, a professor at Perkins School of Theology, wrote a chapter entitled, "Inclusivism, Idolatry and the Survival of the (Fittest) Faithful" in *The Community of the Word*. Upon seeing a T-shirt that read "Embracing diversity is embracing God," he responded with a warning that this kind of belief puts us "on the edge of idolatry."[11]

He goes on to say,

So much good has come out of an inclusion agenda. We all stand in unity on the point that the church must be rid of racism and patriarchy. The question is, "Have we reached a point that the means, in pursuit of the ultimate ends in diversity and inclusion, has become what we worship?"

Inclusion arose as a legitimate effort to implement a glorious vision of equality that is embedded in the gospel; we can be grateful for those theologians, liberal, liberationist and otherwise, who drove home the inclusivist insight. It is now time to get to the news behind the news and work for a change of speech and subject. It was Christ's cross and resurrection that won the victory over exclusion; it is the same cross and resurrection that will heal us of corruption and idolatry carried out under the banner of inclusion.

When it comes our turn to speak, we can change the subject and return to the first order discourse of the gospel. We can immerse ourselves in the great themes

---

[11] William Abraham, "Inclusivism, Idolatry and the Survival of the (Fittest) Faithful," in The Community of the Word: Toward an Evangelical Ecclesiology (Downers Grove: Intervarsity 2005), 137

of the gospel; we can drink afresh from the mercy of God in the cross; we can
ensure that the full faith of the church is tended to and taught; we can lift up
Christ like the serpent in the wilderness and watch him draw all to himself; we
can cry out for a fresh outpouring of the Holy Spirit on the church; we can do
all we can to ensure that the sacraments are duly administered; we can pray
without ceasing for the comprehensive renewal of the whole people of God. The
sharp-edged Word of God is not intimidated by its enemies; it is a healing
Word of truth and salvation.[12]

Remember the purpose for Jesus Christ coming into the world was to save us, and he gave us the church to transform the world and the culture—not to let it bring us to our knees. Let us NOT simply worship inclusivity, diversity, justice, covenant, or unity, or anything that would substitute God in an idolatrous way, nor let us be tricked into bowing at the altar of divisiveness.

Let us passionately worship the God who stands for the good behind all that is godly in inclusivity, diversity, justice, covenant, unity, but never seeks divisiveness.

Hung Up on Jesus

Dr. William Hinson was one of the smartest people I have ever known and a storyteller par excellence. I have been exposed to some of the smartest people I could ever imagine being around, and Bill was second to none intellectually or academically to my professors. In his

---

[12] Ibid., 143-144

Th.D. study days at Emory, he told of a highly respected and beloved bishop in Georgia named Arthur Moore. He was known in his day as King Arthur Moore. Bishop Moore too was a genius and wonderful preacher and orator. Bill said that students would go over to Bishop Moore's house off of the Emory campus and he would spin his wisdom from a rocking chair on his front porch. According to Bill, King Arthur's favorite advice that he would give to seminarians coming his way was to "be very sure about Jesus."

If there was ever a pastor who was sure about Jesus it was my mentor, Bill Hinson. Bill pastored and preached true to his old bishop's advice. I was his associate for seven years, in the mid-1980s and early 1990s, and most of that time my assignment was to coordinate the evangelism efforts of First United Methodist Church in Houston, Texas. Once, a small group of members in the church, most of whom were Bill's age, decided to leave the church and go elsewhere. This is always a painful experience, but it is especially difficult to swallow when it is close friends and confidants. People leaving was a bit unusual in those days at First Church because so many people were joining—nearly seven hundred annually.

One day after worship, Bill asked them why they were considering leaving. One of them replied, "Bill, when you preach, it's 'Jesus, Jesus, Jesus.' You seem to be so hung up on Jesus." Bill just smiled and politely said, "We're going to miss you." What the man didn't realize was that a comment meant as a criticism was music to Bill's ears. Bill looked at me and said, "Brother Copeland, if I could go to my grave and someone would stand and say, 'Lord, he went . . . hung up on Jesus,' it would be enough.'"

My twenty years of pastoral leadership at Lovers Lane has hopefully been true to my convictions of being hung up on Jesus myself. Our mission is "loving ALL people into relationship with Jesus Christ," and if we stay hung up on Jesus, it will be enough. We make music—not like that of cringe-inducing ukuleles, but like a beautiful orchestra— together amidst tension in our local congregation, and the divisive discussion of sexuality is not the main thing. "Loving ALL" and loving them "into relationship with Jesus" is the main thing. If we can't agree that Jesus is the main thing, then togetherness is futile, but I remain hopeful that when we get United Methodists together from around the world, we will hear a vast, sacred harmony singing about Jesus, our Lord and Savior.

Jesus, Spare Us from the Ukuleles

Together

CHAPTER THREE
Moved by the Holy Fence-Mover

By: Stan Copeland

Jesus promised his disciples that God would be with them through the ongoing presence of the Holy Spirit, whose work throughout history has offered both stability and mobility for the people of God.

That same Spirit hovered over the chaos of creation and brought new order into being. God's Spirit filled both the Tabernacle and the Temple as the visible sign of God's presence, to which the people of God could reliably return. The Spirit's descent at Pentecost birthed a church marked from its inception by a unity forged through diversity. The Holy Spirit creates, stabilizes and clarifies God's people.

Yet the Spirit also creates new realities and new understanding. Just prior to his prayer for unity in John 17, Jesus described the work of the Holy Spirit in John 16 as the one who would "declare to you the things to come." The Spirit led Philip to share the good news with an Ethiopian eunuch, spreading the gospel beyond boundaries of race and sexuality. The Spirit also brought Peter the vision of the descending sheet, expanding God's hospitality to the Gentiles.[13]

* * *

The Holy Spirit moved over the chaos of creation and brought about life and order. The Holy Spirit filled both the tabernacle and the temple as the visible sign of God's presence. Jesus promised that the Holy Spirit would come after his ascension into heaven to be God's presence and power with his disciples. The Holy Spirit came upon the believers at Pentecost in the symbols of presence and power—wind

---

[13] "Holy Spirit: Fixed and Free," UnitingMethodists.com/vision

and fire. The Holy Spirit birthed the church of Jesus Christ and marked from its beginning a universal, all-are-welcome diversity.

The Holy Spirit creates, stabilizes, and clarifies God's people. Whether we are talking about Jesus sharing living water with the Samaritan woman who had been married five times, Philip baptizing the Ethiopian eunuch who was seeking to know the ways of God, or Paul baptizing the European woman named Lydia who was a person of prayer, the church was meant for all people and conceived to be diverse. And Peter, the leader of the church, came to understand this as well.

Divisions

More division has taken place over the Holy Spirit and the filling of one with the Holy Spirit than perhaps any other theological belief. So, who can be "holy" and who can be filled with the Holy Spirit? The Methodist Church divided in 1844 largely over issues related to treatment of people of color who were enslaved. The Methodist Church, North and South, splintered over matters concerning the Holy Spirit in the late 1800s. Methodist Churches have since splintered over matters concerning the Holy Spirit and what it means to be "holy" regarding lifestyle—modest dress, speaking in tongues, playing cards, and the like.

"Who can be holy?"

It's a question that has long been an issue for the Judeo-Christian faith. A "holy" lifestyle was in large part determined by what one ate and didn't eat. The dietary laws of Leviticus and Deuteronomy set a distinguishing mark that carried into temple practice. It wasn't just about what one ate, but it also included the sacrifices of animals in the temple. Only animals considered to be clean or those that one could eat and still be holy were acceptable sacrifices.

Who is welcome in the Church of Jesus Christ?

What about Gentiles who desire to be Christians?

These were questions that were central to Christians in the earliest days of the church. All of the earliest Christians were Jews before they became Christians. Even if they were Greek-speaking Hellenistic Jews, they were under the law before they converted to Christianity. The question was, "Do Christ followers need to be under the law?" Today the questions seem to be:

Who can become our brand of Christian?

What is sinful practice?

Today, most would base sinful practice on what the Bible determines to be sin. The problem is that we differ on what the Bible clearly defines as being "sin" and what we have moved beyond to see as "not sin."

I had a breakfast meeting recently with four of our leaders, and three of us sinned, according to Levitical law, by eating bacon and sausage without regret. The holy one in our midst ate turkey bacon, but in my opinion, he was the only one who sinned.

Acts 10:1-16

In Caesarea there was a man named Cornelius, a centurion of the Italian Cohort, as it was called. He was a devout man who feared God with all his household; he gave alms generously to the people and prayed constantly to God. One afternoon at about three o'clock he had a vision in which he clearly saw an angel of God coming in and saying to him, "Cornelius." He started saying to him, "Cornelius." He stared at him in terror and said, "What is it, Lord?" He answered, "Your prayers and your alms have ascended as a memorial before God. Now send men to Joppa for a certain Simon who is called Peter; he is lodging with Simon, a tanner, whose house is by the seaside." When the angel who spoke to him had left, he called two of his slaves and a devout soldier from the ranks of those who served him, and after telling them everything, he sent them to Joppa. About noon the next day, as they were on their journey and approaching the city, Peter went up on the roof to pray. He became hungry and wanted something to eat; and while it was being prepared, he fell into a trance. He saw the heaven opened and something like a large sheet coming down, being lowered to the ground by its four corners. In it were all kinds of four-footed creatures and reptiles and birds of the air. Then he heard a voice saying, "Get up, Peter; kill and eat." But Peter said, "By no means, Lord; for I have never eaten anything that is profane or unclean." The voice said to him again, a second time, "What God has made clean, you must not call profane." This happened three times, and the thing was suddenly taken up to heaven.

Who Are Your Gentiles?

In the scene that follows this passage, Cornelius and Peter meet and share their visions with each other and the audience gathered around them. Then Cornelius begins to worship at Peter's feet. Peter tells him to get up and says, "I am a man like you."

Peter then begins to preach the good news of Jesus Christ. He says, "He is Lord of ALL." While Peter is still speaking, the Gentiles are filled with the Holy Spirit and begin to extol God and speak in tongues. Peter says, "Can anyone withhold baptism from these who have received the Holy Spirit?"

Absolutely not!

We Gentiles have long since been included and the Holy Spirit opened the door and baptism marked us as "family inside the house."

Who are our Gentiles today?

I'm talking about those whom you really wonder if they can be part of us. Who are those whom you doubt that the Holy Spirit would ever fill? Who are your Gentiles?

We need to know that when God's Kingdom comes—and it is coming—division among earth's people, contention and war, competition and racial prejudice, and distrust will come to an end. This is a truth we see evident throughout scripture:

Isaiah saw the deliverer coming "to gather all nations and tongues" (Isa 66:18);

Jeremiah envisioned the time when all nations will gather at Jerusalem (Jer 3:17);

Micah announced that many nations will "go up to the mountain of the LORD" (Mic 4:2);

Zechariah knew that Gentiles seeking God's favor will "take hold of a Jew, grasping his garment and saying, 'Let us go with you, for we have heard that God is with you.'" (Zec 8:20-23).

Jesus seemed to make his point of inclusion by mixing with the Samaritans as depicted in the story of the Woman at the Well (John 4);

Peter saw baptism as the great sign of inclusion as we have just read in the Cornelius story.

Again, who are the Gentiles who God is now asking you to include in a prophetic way?

Moving the Fence

A hand-me-down tale that I love and don't know how to credit is about an American soldier who died of his wounds in France in the First World War. His comrades took him to a small church and asked the village priest if they could bury him in the parish graveyard. "Was he a Catholic?" asked the priest. "No, Father, he was not," replied the men. "Then you must bury him outside the fence of the cemetery," answered the priest. The fallen man was buried just as they were instructed, outside the fence.

His comrades returned the next morning to pay their last respects. They were surprised to see that the fresh grave was within the cemetery fence. They summoned the priest, who said, "My conscience bothered me last evening; I could not sleep so I arose in the night and moved the fence to include your comrade who died for France." Christ died for all people and moved the fence for sinners like you and me.

Mis-Using the Bible

The church has been dividing itself for a long time, and the Bible is consistently misused to accentuate the differences, define the sin, and justify positions.

We seem to be ignoring many of the Levitical laws as Scripture instructs because the Holy Spirit moved the fence. We do not stone, on their father's doorstep, young women who marry and are not virgins. The law instructs us to do that, but the Holy Spirit moved the fence. We do not sacrifice animals as the Bible instructed, instead the Holy Spirit let the prophet Micah move the fence to a matter of the heart: to do justly, to love mercy, and to walk humbly with God. Jesus healed on the Sabbath even though the scripture would count that a sin, so the Holy Spirit moved the fence. Paul welcomed the uncircumcised because God called them clean, and the Holy Spirit had already moved the fence.

Our fences, our walls, are meant to separate and differentiate. It just seems to me that the Holy Spirit moves fences in order to define who can be holy and brings unity through the mark of holiness, doing justly, loving mercy, and walking humbly with God.

Moved by the Holy Fence-Mover

Together

CHAPTER FOUR

Learning to Share the Road

By: Scott Gilliland

While many have debated the degree of the outside culture's influence on the church, we ought also to focus on the culture we create within the church. How do we create a culture rooted in generous and refining grace within the church? We have all been responsible for how division and polarization has shaped our interactions with others in the church.

We are all called to repent of that sin. By God's grace in Christ alone, we can and must seek the holiness that can only come through our common witness and united spirit. We must watch for and participate in the unifying work of the Holy Spirit that creatively shapes and reshapes the way we perceive and relate to each other, demanded of us by Scripture's witness. There is no room for humiliation, dehumanization, or self-righteousness in the church.

Regardless of our starting point in this or any other polarizing debate, the Holy Spirit is always refining and renewing us. The Spirit leads us communally and individually to positions that we would not have claimed before. By the power of the Spirit, the church can be a community of love that holds the space open for individuals to be on their own journey of prayerful self-examination.[14]

* * *

What is a United Methodist?

Is a United Methodist a traditionalist? Someone who is committed to the traditions and essential orthodoxy of the Christian church?

---

[14] "The Church: Fixed and Free," UnitingMethodists.com/vision

Is a United Methodist a progressivist? Someone who is committed to prophetically leading for social justice in our communities and in our world?

Is a United Methodist a centrist? Someone who is committed to the grounded life of individuals and the contexts in which they live?

I think the answer to all three is yes.

The point being, we have a big tent in The United Methodist Church and in the Wesleyan tradition. In our denomination, we seem to have intentionally wide lanes in terms of what we can believe and still call ourselves "United Methodist."

Having just gone through the experience of interviewing with our Board of Ordained Ministry, I knew that in each interview room sat colleagues who held differing views on:

- Historical accuracy of the Old Testament
- Virgin birth
- Bodily resurrection
- Legitimacy of other religions
- Any number of social issues

Suffice it to say, in terms of what we believe, the lanes are wide in our denomination as it is.

But in terms of how we practice ministry, we have narrowed the lanes more and more since our creation in 1968. We keep adding ink to our Book of Discipline in an effort to strictly define how UM pastors ought to practice, regardless what we actually believe.

And so we have a dissonant reality in our church today. We have wide lanes in terms of belief and increasingly narrow lanes in terms of practice and ministry. And it just isn't sustainable.

Same Thing, Different Millenia

As previously stated in this book, the debates surrounding inclusion of LGBTQ persons are symptoms of a deeper divide in our denomination. One of those deeper divides is in our theology of church, specifically whether we should be a denomination of wide lanes or narrow lanes.

This divide is nothing new, as you might have guessed. By chapter fifteen in the book of Acts, we find the early church in heated debate at the Council of Jerusalem, arguing over the narrow lane of circumcision as a practice in historical Judaism and early Christianity.

On one side: A group of traditionalists who were afraid of losing their Jewish identity, demanding all new male believers—including non-Jews—abide by the Jewish custom of circumcision.

One the other side: A group of progressivists, helmed by Peter (a traditionalist whose heart was changed through relationship with

Cornelius, as we saw in the previous chapter) who believed Gentiles ought to be included and offered grace to live outside the narrow lanes that previously defined the Jewish people.

Jesus's influence on Judaism had already widened the lanes of belief for early Jewish Christians, inviting ALL people of the world to be saved through faith in God; and, in fact, you could say Gentile influence had widened the lanes of belief as well. We see this evidenced by Greek philosophical ideas permeating the Gospels, specifically the Gospel of John, and its uplifting of the Greek concept of *logos* or "The Word."

And so we have this debate, which ought to sound familiar: Should Christianity stick to its traditionalist heritage, or should it move forward?

Acts 15:7-11 says this:

> *After there had been much debate, Peter stood up and said to them, "My brothers, you know that in the early days God made a choice among you, that I should be the one through whom the Gentiles would hear the message of the good news and become believers. And God, who knows the human heart, testified to them by giving them the Holy Spirit, just as he did to us; and in cleansing their hearts by faith he has made no distinction between them and us. Now therefore why are you putting God to the test by placing on the neck of the disciples a yoke that neither our ancestors nor we have*

been able to bear? On the contrary, we believe that we will be saved through the grace of the Lord Jesus, just as they will."

The Progressivist Plea

Peter is laying out a classic four-part argument for inclusion that we have seen repeated throughout history for all groups of people (race, gender, ability, etc.).

First, a personal testimony. Peter explains his journey from his traditionalist view to now holding a progressive perspective. **". . . you know that in the early days God made a choice among you, that I should be the one through whom the Gentiles would hear the message of the good news and become believers."** Peter entered the Gentile community as a traditionalist outsider, but left it him changed. Today, we have heard many Christians—clergy and laity alike—express a similar change of heart over the last forty years as they have moved to a more progressive stance on inclusion-related debates.

Second, a witness of the Holy Spirit. Peter testifies to seeing the Holy Spirit at work in the Gentile believers, despite their "unholy" living as uncircumcised. **"And God, who knows the human heart, testified to them by giving them the Holy Spirit, just as he did to us."** For many United Methodists, it has been the personal fellowship and friendship with LGBTQ Christians that has led to heart change, whether that is a beloved family member coming out or witnessing the Holy Spirit at work through LGBTQ Christians in their churches and communities.

Third, a rejection of human judgment. Peter reminds his listeners something Jesus taught time and time again—that we frequently fall into the trap of sitting on the throne of judgment, when that is not our role to occupy. **". . . and in cleansing their hearts by faith [God] has made no distinction between [Gentiles] and us. Now therefore why are you putting God to the test by placing on the neck of the disciples a yoke that neither our ancestors nor we have been able to bear?"** Peter knows that any time we demand "outsiders" to look, live, and express their faith exactly like us, we assume a mantle that is not ours to bear.

Lastly, a call to unity around Christian mission. Peter tries to land on a unifying plea to remember our primary purpose for existing as the church universal. **"On the contrary, we believe that we will be saved through the grace of the Lord Jesus, just as they will."** Peter is reminding the hearers of our common mission as disciples: to share the good news of salvation through faith in Jesus Christ. And look where that mission had taken them—to a new population of people who received the good news and lived in faithful relationship with God without transforming into traditionalist Jews! The urge to assimilate new groups into the dominant group is nothing new; one need only look at the historical church's treatment of women, persons of color, persons with disabilities . . . the list goes on.

The Traditionalist Response

Peter's argument is heard and accepted by the Council, and then James offers his judgment on behalf of the Council. James could be considered a devout traditionalist. In the Letter of James, he defends holiness in action so much that he is accused of supporting works-righteousness by theologians throughout history; and, in fact, Martin Luther considered removing James's epistle from the canonized Protestant Bible for this very reason.

How will this traditionalist respond to Peter's progressive plea?

We hear this in Acts 15:13-20.

After they finished speaking, James replied, "My brothers, listen to me. Simeon has related how God first looked favorably on the Gentiles, to take from among them a people for his name. This agrees with the words of the prophets, as it is written,

'After this I will return,
and I will rebuild the dwelling of David, which has fallen;
from its ruins I will rebuild it,
and I will set it up,
so that all other peoples may seek the Lord—
even all the Gentiles over whom my name has been called.
Thus says the Lord, who has been making these things known from long ago.'

Therefore I have reached the decision that we should not trouble those Gentiles who are turning to God, but we should write to them to abstain only from things polluted by idols and from fornication and from whatever has been strangled and from blood."

James does two really important things here.

First, he acknowledges and supports Peter's testimony and uplifts Scripture that does the same. It is so important in our current conversations to acknowledge that both progressivists and traditionalists recognize the authority of Scripture. It may seem tempting to claim the Bible as "clearly" supporting only one conclusion in debates around sexual ethics and social inclusion, but that claim requires us to overestimate our handle on biblical scholarship while also discounting the Holy Spirit's role in revealing Scripture to each individual who reads it.

Second, at the end of his response, he makes a critical turn: "but we should write to them." The "them" is the church in Antioch, which had a bustling community of Gentile Christians. He is saying, in effect, "We embrace you as fellow Christians, AND we are asking you to be conscious of your Jewish brethren and have compassion that they do not share your more progressive views."

The things he forbids them from are common practices at pagan temple feasts: idolatry, temple prostitution, and unclean food practices.

Obviously, the dietary rules are not law for all churches. Paul acknowledges as much in his letter to the Romans, but Paul says something similar to James.

Essentially, James is asking that in our effort to meet the Holy Spirit with new people in new places, we must also consider and have compassion for those who simply do not share our views on faithful Christian practice.

I agree with Peter's passion, and I agree with James's considerations. We ought to be a church with wide lanes, both in doctrine and practice, knowing that it generates both organizational challenges and vital dialogue as a denomination. But we need to be a church that knows how to share the road, as well as a church that doesn't demand all people everywhere think, pray, and act just like I do in my context or you in yours.

Can we have the freedom to do ministry the way that God has called and confirmed in us and others like us? AND can we allow communities who are tentative to leave their traditionalism the freedom to maintain historical practices that best meet their contextual needs today?

Is God Ever Surprised?

From a sermon by Stan Copeland, delivered at Lovers Lane on January 28, 2018

At times I imagine the church is a disappointment to God, but theologically I have a hard time thinking of the church ever surprising God. I want to tell you about a relationship that is on my mind and in my heart. I want to say I prayed a lot about whether to share this with you. I pray that in you hearing it you hear the heart of a pastor simply sharing and not "preaching" about how you should believe or what is "right" for you. There is not enough honesty in our world today; and, friends, we have to deal with these matters honestly and not say "I'm leaving the church if . . ." There is not enough honesty in our pulpits and too much false pretense concerning what is "right" on difficult matters of consideration. And there's not enough listening.

Before the 2016 General Conference, there was a wedding in Columbus, Ohio, of a United Methodist Ordained Elder and his partner of nearly three decades. It was in a United Methodist Church and officiated by United Methodist pastors, and after that event "holy hell" broke loose over this violation of the Book of Discipline. The man at the center of the controversy was the Reverend David Meredith.

When I went to seminary in Kansas City, Tammy and I had been married just three short weeks, and we were in a strange land making new friends, all of whom were pursuing the call of God to be United Methodist pastors. If ever there was a display of the tent being large, it was in the diversity of theology among my colleagues. David was among them. He was from Ohio, and I resonated with him theologically because in his faith and deep in his spirituality he was theologically conservative (I have quit saying *orthodox*, which means "right" or "true," because it assumes all others are *unorthodox*, or "wrong" and "false"). The joy of the Lord in his heart came through in the countenance of his great big smile. He also had a Wesleyan bent toward social holiness and works of justice that I admired. One of our seminary colleagues said, "None of us loves Jesus more than David."

David was smart, too, and quickly became nearly every teacher's pet because of his good work and keen intellect. There was a group of us who became fast friends, studied together, and socialized with each other. In our group it became apparent that David and a dear friend of ours from Oklahoma, Carol, were getting quite close. It seemed romance was in the air for both of them. They were getting serious when David came to the "painful reality at that time" that though they loved each other, he and Carol could not be a couple because David came to terms with his homosexuality. He shared his realization that he was gay. All of us, our friends, came around David (and Carol). We loved David through the painful, and eventually, freeing reality of his coming out. But what was he to do with his "call" and pursuit of ordained ministry in light of our law that would forbid him to be ordained if he "practiced homosexuality"? What a struggle!

Here's the quandary that has always been with me due to my relationship with David. There seemed to be no one any more called or equipped for ministry than David. If it was, in fact, God who called

David into ordained United Methodist ministry, you know the natural questions one would have to ask:

1) Did God not actually call David and he just misunderstood his calling? And were we all fooled?

2) Was God just as surprised as David was in discovering his homosexual orientation? Can anyone really surprise God?

3) Or could it be that God knew David was gay before David knew that he was gay—and called him nonetheless?

These are my questions.

David did get ordained. I have witnessed his thirty-five years of very effective ministry in The United Methodist Church. He's been an all-star. David later found a partner, and he and Jim have been together for twenty-eight years in a monogamous, covenantal, loving relationship. Our group of friends vacationed together for ten years, meeting somewhere for a week, catching up on life, loving each other as friends, and remembering our seminary days that connected us. The last time we got together, kids were part of this group by now, and I remember we were going to be in Michigan that year on beautiful Walloon Lake. For various reasons, our friends couldn't make the trip, but Tammy and I, along with our kids, Zach and Emily, spent a week together with David and Jim, and what a great time we had.

In 2016, on the eve of The United Methodist Church's General Conference in Portland, Oregon, Tammy and I were invited to David and Jim's wedding. Tammy and I knew that they were to be married in a United Methodist Church, which was against the Book of Discipline. We knew that other clergy would be there. All of these facts made me uncomfortable because I was committed—and still am committed—to uphold the law of our church, whether I agree with it or not, but this was David and Jim, whom we had loved for more than three decades. We went, and the only other one of our friends who could make it was Carol. Tammy, Carol, and I sat in the balcony of a beautiful downtown Columbus United Methodist Church that was packed with friends and members of David's former and present churches. Seventy-five pastors and colleagues were present. And it was an incredible worship service with choirs and beautiful liturgy that brought tears to our eyes, and a mixture of pain and joy that is hard for me to explain.

Some might say, "Why did you go to the wedding and participate in an act that was a 'law breaker'?" I can only say that I have loved, admired, and respected David's call to ministry even before he, or we, knew that he was gay, and I believe God knew all along. God wasn't surprised. I have witnessed David's love for Jim and Jim's love for him for three decades. And I was invited because we are dear friends.

So I just ask you, "Would you have gone?" Some may say no and that is okay. I certainly understand. It is a big tent and room for different convictions, but for Tammy and me, it seemed like yes was the answer and the right and loving thing to do. No regrets!

Learning to Share the Road

Together

CHAPTER FIVE
Who's Water and Table Is It, Anyway?

By: Stan Copeland

The Christian forces must unite on a much more comprehensive scale, and this at an accelerated pace, for if we perpetuate the luxury and inefficiency of our divisions, we shall surely miss the day of our visitation and the realization of our largest possibilities. Is there any reason that can stand before the bar of experience, of sound and unselfish judgment, and of sensitive conscience why the Christian forces of today should not unite and concentrate as never before on the areas of population and of human relationships which have not been brought under the sway of Christ?

Only as we thus transcend our denominational, party, national, and racial boundaries and barriers can we hope to fulfill the mandate of our Lord . . . The time is ripe for a great and striking emphasis upon the Kingdom of God as preached by Jesus. The Christian emphasis shall be truly relevant to present-day needs and conditions, which shall dominate all other considerations and incentives, and which shall become contagious and irresistible. This light of Christian unity is a beacon that draws people to Christ.[15]

* * *

The severity and weariness of our disagreements over human sexuality lead some in the church to see separation as the only possible resolution. Some feel like a "divorce" is the healthiest and most sensible outcome, so that both sides can pursue ministry as they discern it.

A pastor friend, who had gone through a divorce, testified to how he, his ex-wife, and their children live out this new reality. He said, "Even

---

[15] Delivered by John R. Mott at 1939 Uniting Conference, Kansas City, Missouri. John Mott was a Methodist layperson and Nobel Peace Prize Winner.

in the wake of a divorce, where ex-spouses consider their marriage to be irrevocably separated, it is the children of that divorce who must reimagine the unity of their family, and push all of its members to consider new ways that they are still one family together."Who will be the children speaking for unity of family in the midst of separation, and what will The United Methodist Church family look like after 2019?

Hard-Won and Grace-Drenched

When the Apostle Paul wrote to the church in Ephesus, he wrote to a congregation struggling with the challenges that come with ministry in a diverse context, namely the challenge of remaining united in mission and purpose despite disagreements over certain "non-essential" beliefs or values.

In the fourth chapter of his letter to the Ephesians, Paul says this on the subject of unity:

> *I therefore, the prisoner in the Lord, beg you to lead a life worthy of the calling to which you have been called, with all humility and gentleness, with patience, bearing with one another in love, making every effort to maintain the unity of the Spirit in the bond of peace. (Eph 4:1-3)*

The Apostle's words are convicting. The Fruit of the Spirit that he lifts up in Galatians—humility, gentleness, patience, love—are not easy to live out, especially when dealing with conflict in the church. What's more, he tells us we need *all* humility, *all* gentleness, *all* patience, *all* love . . . not just a bit of it, not just what we think we can muster, but *all*.

Have we, as he says, "made every effort" to maintain our unity with *all* gentleness, patience, and love? Some would say yes. And they are likely weary of decades of battling, and have given up hope that this impasse can be resolved without large-scale schism. But there are many, especially amongst our younger leaders—lay and clergy alike—who believe that perhaps we've made every effort at being right or "winning" for "our side," but we have yet to "make every effort at maintaining the unity of the Spirit in the bond of peace."

The truth is, unity is never easy. We usually only talk about being united when there are reasons we ought to be divided in the first place! In this world, unity is hard-won and grace-drenched. Paul makes a case for a unity that is worth fighting for, and must be won, and he reminds us that true unity is only possible through the work of the Holy Spirit drenching our efforts together with grace that has healing in its wings.

As soon as Paul uplifts unity as a virtue worth fighting for, he is wise to quickly remind the church that unity is not for our sake, but rather for the sake of the gospel.

WannaKnowWhy.com

More than a decade ago, Lovers Lane launched an ad campaign that was produced in house by some of our gifted laity and funded by a few believers in the project. It was called "WannaKnowWhy.com" where we shared the stories of our members finding a home at Lovers Lane. Billboards around the Dallas area featured a face of one of our members and a short quote that inspired drivers to go to the website and read their stories. Two stories in particular changed our church more than we could ever have anticipated.

One of the stories featured Peter, who was a refugee immigrant from Liberia. He had a harrowing story of surviving a firing squad and being dumped on a beach with dozens of lifeless bodies. The next day, he made his way to his home only to find that it had been burned to the ground and his wife, Betty, and their five children were gone. Neighbors said they thought they had all been killed.

Peter escaped to a refugee camp and eventually found his way to Dallas. More than two years later, it was reported that Betty and the children had been seen in another refugee camp. During this time, each had thought the other to be dead. Miraculously, the family was reunited in Dallas. Together, they started attending Lovers Lane and joined in 1995. The WannaKnowWhy.com billboard that featured him read, "You can find your sanctuary in ours. Wanna know why?"

Amazing things started to happen. First, African immigrants from all over the DFW metroplex began showing up to Lovers Lane, trusting that they, too, could find sanctuary at our church. Some were Liberians who had been in warring factions in their homeland and were now being reconciled and worshipping together at Lovers Lane. Secondly, the power of the Internet brought the story all the way to a former general in the Liberian army who had ordered the genocidal shooting of Peter and others. The general went to a Lutheran church in Monrovia, where during the civil war it was said that bodies were stacked on the pews. There he repented of his murderous actions, confessed Jesus as his Lord, and was baptized. Months later, the general and Peter became friends—brothers—and visited together upon Peter's return trips back to Monrovia, where he has started a life-saving more-than-one-hundred bed hospital in his home county of Nimba in Zoe Geh among the Geo people.

Another one of the WannaKnowWhy.com stories featured a member of our church who is a medical doctor named Jim. He shared his relief at finding a church that would welcome him as a gay man. He talked about how since he was a youth he had been made to feel unwelcome in churches because of who he was, and how for the first time he had found a church that offered a "you are welcome" hospitality for him, his partner, and their two daughters. They had their twin daughters baptized at Lovers Lane by Dr. Bill Bryan, then the Sr. Pastor. Jim's partner wrote this to me when the girls graduated high school. I was privileged to read this letter a few years later at his memorial service held recently at Lovers Lane.

Dear Stan,

Our daughters are just now finishing up their last week of high school. How hard is it to believe that they are now seventeen—almost eighteen—at this point? On Wednesday, they will graduate from Plano West High School. Jim and I are a little more than breathless and speechless about this part of their lives . . . and more than over the top about their accomplishments so far in their short lives.

The girls were five months old when they were baptized at our church, not without a little more than an uproar, on 12-24-95. We took those vows very seriously—much to the shock of the very (then!) conservative and very full 9:30 a.m. Christmas Eve congregation. . . I think we have seen a lot of changes in those seventeen-plus years. Jim and I are very proud and pleased that both ladies do rely on their faith when they need to; not as much as we would like, yet we know they are teenagers. We know that they have a great foundation, thanks to Lovers Lane.

I thank you on behalf of my family for the welcoming home LLUMC has provided for Jim, me, and the girls. We have always felt so very welcomed and loved.

With love,
Lar

That baptism in particular had something to do with me coming to Lovers Lane two short years later, when Dr. Bryan was appointed to Perkins School of Theology. The baptism controversy—which made the local magazine—was still being talked about when I arrived as pastor. I have come to believe that Bill Bryan's convictions laid the groundwork for what Lovers Lane has come to be.

Shortly after Jim's story was featured on WannaKnowWhy.com, and the gay community of Dallas read the witness that Lovers Lane was a welcoming place, we had LGBTQ people showing up, ready to join and to get baptized. The word was contagious: The church loved them as they were! Friendship evangelism happened like never before. It was like the old evangelical saying: "one beggar telling another beggar where to find bread."

WannaKnowWhy.com caused us to have to decide what kind of church we would be. People at that time joined Lovers Lane after taking a class and sharing one-on-one with a pastor who heard their story and tried to get them involved in ministry and a group. In other words, joining the church was intentional and the choice was prayerfully made. I like to say about that era that "no one was sneaking in."

I was personally warned by a few of my theologically conservative colleagues and friends that allowing LGBTQ people to join and receive the sacrament of baptism would be the end of our congregation. One well-meaning friend told me, "THEY will split your congregation in half and THEY will not stay." It turned out to be quite the opposite.

We had people seeking baptism like never before, and they were primarily coming as refugees—whether refugees from countries ravaged by war or "church refugees,"[16] who had been rejected by a church culture that wanted nothing to do with "sinners" like them. The waters of baptism started getting full at Lovers Lane.

Lovers Lane is still growing, with people coming from many different countries in Africa, LGBTQ people, and persons who are deaf or have other physical or mental challenges. Former offenders whom we served in prison come our way upon release. Those recovering from addictions walk across the street from our Center for Spiritual Development, where nearly one thousand persons per week are in groups in our Twelfth Step Ministry. Families come from our affluent North Dallas neighborhoods who are looking for a "different" Christian community where diverse faith expression is appreciated and the vision of Christ for the world.

For the last decade, approximately two-thirds (nearly 70 percent) of our members join by profession of faith. That means we're baptizing a lot of people. At Lovers Lane we use an immersion pool for most of our adult baptisms, and we don't change the water between baptisms! We don't have one pool for Africans and another pool for LGBTQ. We don't have a pool for the deaf and another for the former offender or another for the recovering addict. Furthermore, we do not have a

---

[16] I say this not to equate the horrors of war with the trauma experienced by LGBTQ persons, but only to acknowledge there are similarities in their experience of feeling "threatened" or "pushed out" of their "home."

pool for traditionalists and another pool for progressives, and, well, you get the idea.

We have one pool, one baptism, one faith, one Lord, and one gospel, as Paul reminds us. It's the gospel mission that keeps us united in the midst of our diversity—not only in race and sexuality, but also in ideology, political leaning, socioeconomic status, age, and ability. We claim this diversity-in-unity in our church's vision statement that we can never say enough: *"One diverse community, passionately engaging the Bible, uplifting Jesus in worship and loving service, and challenging in love that which divides."*

Diversity works at Lovers Lane; it defines our mission field. We believe it works in The United Methodist Church, in that we are one of the last mainline churches that has somehow remained together in light of our global nature and our differing beliefs and practices. We maintain that unity will work even better if a gospel focus and evangelistic zeal becomes the "main thing," and we are truly reaching into our defined mission fields to meet people where they are even before they come our way. While we may disagree on lesser points of theology, belief, or practice, surely we could stay united around a mission to reach those whom Christ is leading us to serve with the life-changing gospel of Jesus Christ.

A Young Man's Call to Unity

In the spring of 1939, Tom Shipp (who would later become the first full-time pastor of Lovers Lane) and two other college ministerial students decided to drive to Kansas City for the historic Methodist Uniting Conference. For Tom it was historic for another reason. During the conference, he had an experience that helped him to decide to give his life in the service of God and the Christian Church. Tom later described the moment in the final sermon he would preach on a Sunday before his death that Thursday at Lovers Lane:

It was a great conference. I particularly remember one evening when John R. Mott, one of the great Methodist laymen, gave a sermon. At the close of his message, he gave an invitation to the youth who were there to come forward if they wanted to dedicate their life to full-time Christian service. I got up and walked down the aisle, along with a great number of other young men and women. At the time I wanted more than anything else to have some unique place in the service of the Christian church. I was hungry and open to know all that I could about God and what was happening.

Thank God for the 1939 Uniting Conference and the inspiration to a youth who was there whom God called into ministry to be a beacon, a light, a city set on a hill. He heard his call and came to Dallas for seminary. He also made an impact on Dallas and the world through his leadership in recovery ministry, especially assisting those dealing with alcoholism. He was willing to be radically welcoming to all.

All he wanted to do was build a church where there would be "no shams, no make believe, no halfway measures . . . true friends of others and loyal to Jesus." And people came, and they came, and they came, to the point that Lovers Lane was 8,200 members in 1968 and the fourth largest Methodist church in the country. In 1968, Tom Shipp and Lovers Lane helped host the last Uniting Conference here in Dallas, when the Methodist Church united with the Evangelical United Brethren Church forming The United Methodist Church.

An Orphan Pastor

On World Communion Sunday in October 1970, Tom Shipp shared his story. Tom Shipp was, in essence, an orphan. His mother died when he was four years old, leaving him and four siblings with their father. They moved from New Mexico where they were living back to Missouri, which was their home. His father worked for the railroad, and he could not care for them during the Great Depression. When Tom's beloved grandmother died, all of the children found themselves living with other families. Tom grew up living in the barns and extra rooms of Missouri farmers, working for room and board while going to school.

Tom gave his congregation a personal glimpse into the austerity of his life during this difficult period when he was growing up as an orphan in the homes and barns of farming families. The two families with whom he lived as a high school student had different perspectives on life, faith, and Tom. Tom told this story nearly fifty years ago:

I had just secured a place to live and a place to work. I arrived in the afternoon, put my belongings on the back porch, went with the man of the house to do the chores, and before they were finished night had almost fallen. I washed my face and hands at the well . . . came to the kitchen . . . walked in . . . time for supper. Everyone walked into the dining room to eat, and I followed. When everyone was seated, it was obvious that all the places had been taken. Everything grew silent as I stood. And then the man spoke up and said, "Boy, you don't eat at this table. It's for us. When we're finished, you'll be given a plate. You may eat at the stool and the bench that's on the back porch." My place to sleep was the barn. This I did for more than a year.

Then came the time when I decided this was no longer a place for me to live or to work. My dad made arrangements for me to move in with a neighbor not far away, and he secured a place for me to live. And it was different then. Now I was able to be a part of the family. A giving, churchgoing family. I was seated at the table and slept in the house. They gave me my first new pair of shoes and set of clothes. They loved me and made me feel like one of them.

Then came the time for church, and I was granted the privilege to go. I was even given some money to place on the altar rail for Holy Communion, as I didn't have any money to my name. Oddly enough, both these families belonged to the same Methodist church. Strange things seem to happen, and God lets strange things happen. The first Sunday I attended church it was communion. The ushers directed people to the communion table. The family I was with insisted that I go with them. (I had remained seated.) Strangely enough, the communion rail reached all around the front of the church. And strangely enough, as I knelt down, the man I had worked for knelt down beside me on my right, and the man for whom I was now working was at my left (Mr. Les Kuhn).

The communion elements were served. And the man at my right, for whom I had worked, took my hand and held it just as I reached for the bread. I can still feel the tension. The man to my left was Mr. Kuhn, and his face turned bright red. I can still hear the words that he said as he leaned forward, the preacher still holding the elements, not moving. He said to the man, "It's not your table!" There was a hush that came over the whole sanctuary. "It's not your table! It's not your table!" Finally, before matters came to blows, the man released his grip, and I was allowed to take Holy Communion for the first time.

"It's Not Your Table"

Story can bring unity and nothing speaks to unity like the Lord's Table and Holy Communion with an open invitation.

There is no doubt that Tom Shipp left his mark on Lovers Lane in the thirty-one years he was the pastor in charge. He brought to the office of pastor his story and the lessons he was learning along the way. I believe "It's not your table" rang in the ears of Tom Shipp the rest of his life and helped to form this local congregation and centered our ministry and worship on ALL people having a place at the Lord's Table. At the Lord's Table, ALL are welcome, and it is our sacred duty to make sure that the world knows it.

The growth and development of Lovers Lane, like all churches, is not the work of one pastor, or two, or three, or four, or the dozens of wonderful staff, pastors, and ministers. Lovers Lane is what it is largely because of the people who God brings together, and they are quite the diverse collection of God's children. And when the congregation comes forward for the Lord's Supper at the Lord's Table, it is a portrait of unity in diversity that is hard-won and grace-drenched. Paul continues his witness to the Ephesians and to United Methodists today with these words:

> *There is one body and one Spirit, just as you were called to the one hope of your calling, one Lord, one faith, one baptism, one God and Father of all, who is above all and through all and in all.* (Eph 4:4-6)

Who's Water and Table Is It, Anyway?

Together

CHAPTER SIX
At Times, It's Tough Being a Pastor

What "The Table" Teaches Me

By: Scott Gilliland

When I first heard the story that Stan shared of Tom Shipp's life-changing communion experience, I remember simply being awed. How this one act of kindness on the part of Mr. Kuhn in a little Missouri Methodist church came to impact the vision and culture of a large church in Dallas almost a century later still leaves me breathless, even after hearing the tale a dozen times. As I consider this story now, especially in light of the tensions present in our larger denomination, it makes me pause and reflect in new ways.

First, I am struck by the experience Tom had in the two homes he worked in as a boy. In the first home, Tom's presence is viewed by the father as a liability, an unfortunate necessity, and Tom is reminded regularly, through word and action, that he is not a member of the family. He is fed, but not at the table. He is housed, but in the barn. In short, he is tolerated.

I do not think anyone enjoys feeling tolerated. I think about debates that grip our denomination currently, and I hear a lot of discussion around the importance of tolerance, as though tolerating people you would really rather not be present is somehow a fulfillment of the

73

gospel that Jesus preached. The truth is, people know when they are welcomed and when they are tolerated, and if Tom's life is any indication, being tolerated only drives people away, but being welcomed will transform their whole world. I look at the church universal today, and I see a lot of people who are tolerated, allowed to eat (but on the porch), allowed to rest (but in the barn), and allowed to be in church (but with limitations). To put it simply: If we want people in our family, we need to stop tolerating them and start welcoming them, or else they will decide for themselves that this family is not for them.

Second, I have some holy envy of Tom's experience as a young man discerning God's call on his life in the era of denominational uniting. Tom would die only nine years after witnessing the uniting conference of The United Methodist Church in 1968, and meanwhile I am just beginning a life of ministry while our denomination dances on the brink of schism. How hopeful it must have been for Tom to hear God calling him to ministry as Methodists found more and more reasons to be together despite inevitable differences. In the midst of our denominational debates, I hope we do not forget that the children, youth, and young adults both inside and outside the UMC are watching and judging our witness. They watched their parent's generation's divorce rate skyrocket, so they are marrying later and less often. They watch elected officials and political pundits endlessly yell across aisles, so they are voting less than any generation before. Will they see the nuance of a church that cannot reconcile differing doctrines? Will they understand the issues of conflicting biblical interpretations, or will they simply see yet another group of people who cannot figure out how to live together? And will they disengage from us the same way they have disengaged from those things that are disappointingly divided?

Lastly, everybody wants to belong. We don't just go to the gym—we "join" a gym. We don't just shop for groceries—we become a "member" of the local store and gain access to those exclusive deals that only people with the fortitude to fill out a short questionnaire receive. And when I first heard the story of Tom Shipp at the communion railing, what struck me was how much it must have meant to him to know that, in that moment, he belonged somewhere. He belonged in the loving grasp of a father figure who met him with grace where he had previously been met with contempt, and he belonged at the communion table in the loving grasp of God the Father whose grace lit a fire in that young orphan boy's belly.

* * *

From a Pastor's Heart

By: Stan Copeland

Let me share my heart and more personally. For thirty-five years I have been a United Methodist pastor, and I have a dozen or so years before retirement. My son-in-law, J. B., is a fresh seminary graduate and excitedly aspiring to be a United Methodist pastor. I had the honor to baptize him five years ago on Easter Sunday.

J. B. is the prime example of the people we are trying to reach. He grew up in the church but was not committed to the church of that denomination with theology that he questioned. He was a true seeker, a bit conservative politically and theologically, and socially he was a typical millennial who wondered why his newfound denomination was so hung up on the sexuality of individuals. He just wanted to love and serve Jesus (a bit more theological-seminary-trained sophisticated), and the Lord spoke to his heart about a call to ministry.

A "Nativist" Christianity?

Lately, I've been thinking about the negatives of being referred to as a *Christian pastor*. To many secular people, to be "Christian" is to be separatist, bigoted, and, some believe, just plain hateful. These are unfair labels, but to a world of people whom we are commissioned to "love into relationship with Jesus" and ultimately "transform into Christ's love in action," we have some work to do.

Whatever their politics, many admire our former president George W. Bush for his humble Christian walk. Recently, he used the word "nativism" in reference to a concern he has for our country. According to dictionary.com, nativism is an ideology of "protecting the interests of native-born or established inhabitants against those of immigrants." President Bush was making a point that nativism is not what it means to be an American. Could it be that nativism is also in drastic contrast to our Judeo-Christian biblical mandates regarding the "stranger" and the hospitality we are called to share?

When Christianity sounds like an exclusive religious club we miss the mark with the increasing masses that observe what they see as the "nativist" Christian stance: "If you're in the club, we want to support you, and if you're not in the club, forget it."

There are many Christians who are quick to tell you who is going to hell and who isn't, who's holy and who is not. There are many Christians today who believe the way that you vote or your political views must be a certain way on a number of issues or your salvation is in question. The description of evangelical that I have proudly owned has come primarily to be political terminology, and that has never been more true than it is today. Being a little "left" of center politically, I started calling myself a Wesleyan Evangelical to underscore my traditional Arminian theology and Wesley's spirit of reaching out to a world in need. When I see pastors proudly flying the evangelical banner while degrading God's children of other faiths and those of the LGBTQ community, I want nothing to do with matters of association. When *evangelical* is reduced to sectarian nativism our good word has been hijacked.

I do not sense that kind of blatant separatism coming out of the mouths of my United Methodist colleagues, even my more theologically conservative ones. Still, it is complicated these days to be known as a Christian, and perhaps even more so to be a Christian pastor. And, regrettably, throw the word *evangelical* in the mix and ears close and hearts harden to our message.

Nothing More Sacred

What I know and share with my son-in-law and other young United Methodist pastors is how fulfilling the vocation of Christian pastor has been and still is for me. There is nothing more sacred or awe-inspiring than being with people at the birth of their children. I have even baptized stillborn babies at the request of heartbroken parents, ignoring theological "rightness" involving the act. The love of Jesus and his practice, for me, always trumps dogma.

I share the joy with these budding pastors of serving at the Lord's Table and watching the congregation one-by-one receive the sacrament, knowing some of their deepest secrets and most profound heartaches. There is great joy in baptizing an infant that you hold in your arms or in baptizing an adult who has chosen the God that first chose and loved her or him.

There is nothing I do that I feel more needed in doing than ministry at the time of death or the healing act of a memorial service. Officiating at weddings today is becoming "anybody can do it" with a quick, online certification. However, there are some who love the ritual of Christian marriage that we uniquely share as we point people to the presence of the living Lord who blesses Christian love expressed in marriage.

A Wedding

Sometimes it's such a joy being a Christian pastor, and sometimes it's tough. Often, it is a challenge. Once, a couple, who were very much in love, contacted the church on a Tuesday about getting married at Lovers Lane, their church, on the upcoming Sunday. They had not gone through the traditional channels of counseling and setting up the church in advance for the wedding, in large part because one of them was recently diagnosed with seriously advanced cancer. In light of treatments and matters of dealing with the disease, it was their desire to have the wedding immediately. They were active members at Lovers Lane and our "welcome" had changed their lives. The woman who was diagnosed with cancer wrote this:

A little over a year ago I paced back and forth in the parking lot of our church arguing with God about going in. I had been devastated by my church home almost fifteen years prior. I wasn't ready. I have always loved God, but I wasn't ready for the people in the church. That day I gave it to God and trusted Him. In the last year I have been met with nothing but love and acceptance. Even my children who never wanted to go to church have attended service with us. I have known that our church and congregation as a whole are truly amazing and set aside from so many. I have been the recipient of so many blessings there inside our walls, but also outside our church walls. I'm honored to be part of a church that doesn't just say "we love all" but proves it in every action.

Today, I am overwhelmed by the outpouring of love and support that Lovers Lane has shown us. I will never be able to formulate the correct words of appreciation that we both have. To say thank you seems too simple, but thank you. Thank you for everything. My heart is bursting with all the love I feel, and I am honored that you all love us so much. Thank you for every word. Thank you for every action. Thank you for being the loving hands of God. Thank you for showing me what love truly is and thank you for the healing that each of you has given me through our Lord. I am humbled. Our God is good. He is so very good! Thank you again.

Wow! What do you do with a letter like that? It's hard to contain the pride I have for our church. But it's hard to be a Christian pastor these days.

This letter came after I had to tell her that we couldn't host their wedding at her beloved church because our Book of Discipline won't allow us to have a wedding for two people of the same sex, even though they are in love, and even though the state of Texas will give them a marriage license. What's a Christian pastor to do? This letter came after their humble request not to use any of our chapels or the sanctuary, but rather to have the wedding in a little house and garden on our campus. They understood that none of their pastors could participate, in accordance with the Book of Discipline. They shared that they already had their online certified officiant to perform the wedding.

At Times It's Tough Being a Pastor

The letter came after I had emailed a few of our key leaders, six couples, and shared the joys and challenges of being a United Methodist pastor. I wrote the following:

A United Methodist Pastor cannot officiate at a same-sex wedding according to our Book of Discipline, and the clergy of our church don't disobey the Discipline, but decisions these days for Christian pastors are difficult.

I am very uneasy, even sad to respond to our members, who were both baptized here, having to deny their request. I believe the local churches should be allowed to make these decisions concerning matters that have to do with ministry in their congregations and in keeping with what is appropriate in the respective mission field. Likewise, I will not dismiss or disobey the Book of Discipline, but I long for a local option on these matters.

Bishop McKee (the bishop of the North Texas Annual Conference) allows our clergy to participate in same-sex marriages by offering a prayer and/or a reading, but not the pronouncement or the official signing of the marriage license. Our policy on staff is that if one of us is invited and chooses to participate, we write a letter to the bishop and copy our district superintendent informing them of our participation and that we will abide by the restrictions. Whereas I would never force someone to officiate at a wedding that they had theological problems performing, I would however be in favor of allowing a clergy person to officiate at such a wedding if they were committed to doing so.

While church property could not be used without disobedience regarding the Book of Discipline, what if a member of Lovers Lane offered their property? In

81

other words, what if God was calling a few of our members to avail their home or backyard for a wedding of people of the same sex? I don't even know if this couple would want to accept such an offer, but it would be great to be able to extend such hospitality. Also, I would encourage the couple to use one of our staff members to participate in the service according to the stipulations of participation clearly lined out by our bishop. What do you think about my predicament?

Kindest Regards,
Stan

Each member who received my letter said, in so many words, that they would be happy to host the wedding at their house. One leader, who is an executive in an oil company and proudly has a new shotgun that has the Second Amendment engraved on the barrel (not exactly a "raving liberal"), wrote this:

Stan,

You know our minds and our hearts well. It is our true belief that it is not our place to say, or judge, what is right or wrong with same-sex couples and marriages. Who are we to understand this complex issue of human behavior? That therefore, to us, is one of the easiest decisions for us to understand to be truly in God's hands. We hold this to be true especially— ESPECIALLY—when those couples love God and believe that Jesus Christ is their Lord and Savior. Perhaps, it is the same even if they do not.

At the same time, we understand the conundrum and would never ask, or expect you or any of our pastors to act outside of the directives set forth in the Book of Discipline or by Bishop McKee. To us, your suggestion is a great compromise and one that we support. I expect that many folks will. We also think that any couple who truly has Christian hearts would understand the issue, could see beyond the bigger internal struggle, and would welcome the proposal of an alternative "church" location. We would gladly offer our home for such a wedding.

The pastor's job gets easier when she or he shares the load with the local congregation that they serve. I learned that early in my life through my rural, local United Methodist Church through a little Sunday School class song:

The church is not a building;
the church is not a steeple;
the church is not a resting place;
the church is a people.

And the people have property! When matters move to prayerful consideration and relationships, it seems like God's people often make a way, one that is faithful, practical, and always made in the context of our local setting and unique mission field.

I shared this dilemma that I faced with the church on Sunday morning, realizing the templers and tabernaclers were all there, but I trusted that as we gathered around the Lord's Table we would remember that it's not our table and acceptance and love has to always be our mantra. From the pastor's heart, I shared that Sunday morning in the pulpit everything that I have shared in this chapter. Likewise, I also felt the need to say that some of us, staff and membership, may not agree with my actions or the action of fellow members to invite such a wedding to take place. And that is okay; I'd be glad to talk and pray with any of them. Others will see it as a caring act of compassion, and still others will wonder why we have to make such a big deal out of these matters regarding human sexuality and marriage. I gave the benediction and told the congregation that I was going to a wedding—not just because I was simply invited, but because I am the couple's pastor.

At Times It's Tough Being a Pastor

Together

CHAPTER SEVEN
A Conversation with A Beloved Mentor

By: Stan Copeland

In many places I have led audiences in repeating an important phrase: "the main thing is to keep the main thing the main thing." Doing so leads people to ask "What is the main thing?" and then to focus their time, talents and money on the purpose for which the Church exists. I believe unity is an important part of the "main thing." Living into the gift of unity requires focus on our deepest purpose and what God is doing in our midst.

... I still believe that God and the world need a "united" United Methodist Church and that my basic approach holds the best promise for that. I might summarize this approach as placing a high value on unity for biblical, theological, and missional terms. This does not mean uniformity, and the variety of voices represented in [Staying at the Table] show how much we all need one another to discern God's will for our Church.

... I believe the concluding question of my essay, "How do we live more fully into the gift of unity?" is not susceptible to an easily formulated, once-for-all answer. Rather, it is a guiding question worth asking, and then asking again. God is calling us to unity, mission, and embodying "the faith that was once for all entrusted to the saints" (Jude 3). May God continue to guide the people of The United Methodist Church.

— Bishop Scott Jones, "Staying at the Table: The Gift of Unity for United Methodists" (Nashville: Abingdon Press)

* * *

The Main Thing

Before Bishop Jones was a bishop, when he was a professor of evangelism, I remember him reminding us that *"the main thing is to keep the main thing the main thing."* For me, the main thing is *"lifting high the cross"* that Jesus said would draw all people to God—and all means ALL. Our denomination, as well as every local church that is growing and missional, shares a vision and similar wording about "making disciples of Jesus Christ for the transformation of the world." Whereas there are local churches, United Methodists and others, that do not emphasize a Christo-centric mission, I believe the vast majority of local United Methodist churches embrace and pursue a "making disciples of Jesus" mission.

I have already shared the sadness of my heart at how the world we are trying to transform by the grace of God and the power of the Holy Spirit is quick to dismiss Christians—and quicker to dismiss evangelicals. In an article in *The Atlantic* entitled "The Last Temptation," Michael Gerson outlines the current political scene in the United States, and he makes the case that evangelicals have been hooked into the political wrangling and deep division in our land.[17]

Our country is as divided as perhaps it was in the early 1960s (related to race relations and civil rights) and the 1840s through the 1860s (related to slavery). The church again is in the middle of a larger cultural divide. Gerson names prominent evangelicals (without naming one United Methodist) in making a point that what evangelicals have stood for traditionally has morphed into an obsession with a divisive sociopolitical agenda. It also names and quotes well-known

---

[17] www.theatlantic.com/magazine/archive/2018/04/the-last-temptation/554066/

evangelicals who are challenging fellow evangelicals for selling their souls to political agenda and losing sight of the main thing.

Another insight that merits attention is where younger people, like my children, are today. Gerson said, "Evangelicalism is hardly a monolithic movement. All of the above leaders would attest that a significant generational shift is occurring: younger evangelicals are less prone to political divisiveness and are concerned with social justice. In a poll last summer, nearly half of white evangelicals born since 1964 expressed support for gay marriage." I wonder what the stats on that point alone would be if the search were narrowed to children born when mine were (1980s and 1990s). My guess is that those who claimed to be evangelical in this group would be much smaller. Likewise, the percentage would be much higher of those who support gay marriage and wonder why on earth the church has gravitated so off message.

A Beloved Evangelical Mentor

The first time I can remember calling myself an evangelical, I was on the staff of the First United Methodist Church in Houston. I was an evangelical in practice from my youth, holding youth revivals in my teens and early twenties. I greatly value to this day seeing young people profess their faith in Jesus Christ. In college and seminary, my yellow dog democratic-party supporting upbringing gave me a hunger for social justice that was fed through higher education. I was on my way to earn a Ph.D. in Social Ethics, following my seminary experience in Kansas City and two years of pastoral ministry in East Texas, when my plans were interrupted by a terminal diagnosis of leukemia in March 1986.

In May 1986, I was ordained an elder in The United Methodist Church, and two weeks later I was on Bill Hinson's staff as one of his associates. It was his mentorship and my admiration for his preaching and passion for evangelism that led me to own who I was as an evangelical. Physically, I believe I was healed through the miracle of an experimental drug and measures beyond my understanding, since a very small percentage of people on the drug got positive results. Spiritually, I became very grounded in the work of evangelism and led our evangelism team, which was very lay ministry intensive, at a time when we were bringing in 600–700 people to the church annually.

In my seventh year on staff, I was privileged to start the West Campus of our congregation, and when I left in 1993, we had over six hundred people meeting in a hotel ballroom and dozens of small groups that had been trained in the practice of friendship evangelism. There was nothing that Bill Hinson valued more than seeing one come to faith in Jesus Christ and be baptized. The most important statistic to him that we reported annually was how many adult professions of faith commitments we had that year and how many people were led to Christ through the waters of baptism.

No one preached the cross or lifted it any higher than did my mentor-pastor, Bill Hinson. One of the greatest blessings of my ministry was sitting at his feet for seven years as his Associate Pastor at First

Church, Houston. I liked to think that Bill and I had a "Paul and Timothy" type of relationship, and his counsel and friendship was one of the great gifts of my life. I have missed that counsel every day since his death on December 26, 2004, a month after he suffered a brain stem stroke. One of the greatest heartbreaks I have ever experienced was the news and firsthand realization that he would not survive the brain trauma and I would never talk to him again.

How many times, especially in the last few years have I needed to talk with Bill, especially about my local church and what God was doing at Lovers Lane. I've wanted to share about how many people are coming into membership by profession of faith and through the waters of baptism. Then I would say most of them are African from many different countries and sisters and brothers from the LGBTQ community. I have also had the pressing need to discuss our larger denomination's conflict over human sexuality, a topic that he ably addressed for decades.

I wrote a book entitled *Lord, He Went* about Bill's life, sharing his stories, passions, and convictions. In the book I wrote this, envisioning what Bill might say to us United Methodists,

> *The world is in need of a savior. And we United Methodists are in need of a focus on our mission of "Making Disciples of Jesus Christ," along with our global evangelistic strategies, the atrocities of genocide, starvation, and the world epidemic of AIDS. Furthermore he would espouse that General Conferences could not be effective as long as man saw the "main thing" as divisive social*

agenda and politics related to abortion, stem-cell research, homosexuality, and transgender issues, and so forth. He knew that we are divided on these issues as a country and a church. We need a "main thing" focus on which we can find a greater sense of unity from our Wesleyan theology and heritage.[18]

The 2004 General Conference in Pittsburgh was such a tension-filled time, and Bill was so front and center in his discussion of it being time for an "amicable separation" in United Methodism. He and others of our evangelical tribe believed by this separation that those we now call progressive non-compatibilist (which was considered by many to be less than five percent of the denomination) would leave United Methodism, and the rest of us would focus more on evangelism and mission. It was strong, too strong for most, even amongst his evangelical friends. Few wanted to be seen as "dividers."

On Wednesday night, May 5, 2004, I met Bill for coffee. He shared with me about the speech he was going to deliver the next morning. He was still reeling from a late-night meeting the day before with a few of his colleagues and some others who were on the far left on the matters of homosexuality. He said, "Brother Copeland, we can't continue like this. We are on high-center. We have to move toward some kind of solution. One of my colleagues said last night that 'the culture would bring the church to its knees on the issue of homosexuality so we must go where the culture is taking us.' Brother

---

[18] Stanley R. Copeland, *Lord, He Went* (Nashville: Abingdon Press, 2005), 92

Copcland, I thought the church was in the transformation business, didn't you?"

In the so-called "800 lb. Gorilla speech" delivered to a friendly Confessing Movement crowd, Bill Hinson spoke,

> *No sincere person can rejoice in another person's pain. No one enjoys stepping on another person's dream. [. . .] No earnest Christian enjoys seeing another's human suffering. I believe it is time to end this cycle of pain we are afflicting on each other. I dream of men's, women's, and youth movements grounded in the Great Commission. As someone stated, 'It's not that life is so short, it's that eternity is so long.' There are people out there dying and God wants to use us to share the Good News.*
>
> *We cannot fight both church and culture. Our culture alone confronts us with more challenges than we can, humanly speaking, confront and challenge. That struggle, combined with the continuous struggle in the church, is more than we can bear. And our people, who have been patient, should not have to continue to endure our endless conflict. I believe the time has come when we must begin to explore an amicable and just separation that will free both [sides] from our cycle of pain and conflict.[19]*

I have wanted to have a discussion with Bill like that night over coffee during the General Conference and ask him, now nearly fifteen years later, if our dreams are mutually exclusive. If we evangelicals are first

---

[19] Ibid., 98–99.

and foremost about sharing the Good News to a dying world that we are called to transform by God's grace, are all local church approaches to be the same? And if we realize that the mission field in Snipesville, Georgia, is different than San Francisco, California, and different still in Monrovia, Liberia, are we not all called to evangelize in our local contexts?

Furthermore, if the language that we have been fighting over for fifty years were no more, and the covenant was not broken because we allowed folk to serve with what they see as integrity to the gospel in sharing with those who they are called to serve, could we stay united? What if we knew most congregations, globally and in the United States, would not change their approach regarding homosexuality, but knew more autonomy within the connection was needed? Would we need to amicably separate? I trust my local church's leadership to make decisions that will be true to their mission and vision, and if some can no longer stay in a particular United Methodist church, there is a more progressive or more traditional United Methodist church not far away.

A Letter to my Mentor

Dear Bill,

You have always said that real ministry happens in the local church. If covenant is not broken (due to language in the Book of Discipline being removed), does it impact my local church setting if the Reconciling Congregation up the street three miles does a same-sex wedding? Or if a Confessing Movement congregation passes an ordinance kindly saying we do not allow for same-sex weddings on our campus? And finally, am I doing the right thing at Lovers Lane by baptizing people who are LGBTQ and convincingly sharing that they were born and created by God with sexual attraction and orientation that is different than mine?

I fear that the church has been brought to our knees—not by homosexuality—but by a culture that worships at the altar of divisiveness and "us" and "them." What is the church's most powerful witness, division, or unity in love in the midst of our differences? You are right in saying my generation is the first in our denomination's history not to see growth. I do wonder why, if 1968 was our growth peak and we started adding language regarding homosexuality four years later, if it could be that there is something about a feuding body of Christ that is a major turnoff to the world we are trying to reach for Jesus' sake? Why has our evangelical tribe remained obsessed with language regarding sexuality when there are people yet to reach for Jesus Christ, including those who are LGBTQ?

We need to talk.

In Christ,
Stan

How many times I have longed for that conversation.

Some might say Bill would always side with the traditionalists or evangelicals on this matter, and that might very well be true. The champion I knew in him would listen and would think twice if the division was likely to be more substantial than he believed it would have been in 2004. My beloved mentor would always listen in love and ultimately would gravitate toward his dream of movements of people grounded in the Great Commission.

A Conversation with a Beloved Mentor

Together

CHAPTER EIGHT
An 80-Pound, 97-Year-Old Cross-Lifter

By: Stan Copeland

Lift high the cross, the love of Christ proclaim,
till all the world adore his sacred name.
Led on their way by this triumphant sign,
The hosts of God in conquering ranks combine.

Lift high the cross, the love of Christ proclaim,
till all the world adore his sacred name.
Each newborn servant of the Crucified
bears on the brow the seal of him who died.

Lift high the cross, the love of Christ proclaim,
till all the world adore his sacred name.
O Lord, once lifted on the glorious tree,
As Thou hast promised, draw the world to thee.

Lift high the cross, the love of Christ proclaim,
till all the world adore his sacred name.
So shall our song of triumph ever be:
Praise to the Crucified for victory! [20]

* * *

Ms. Elizabeth

Brother Gilliland, let me introduce you to a member of Lovers Lane named Elizabeth Price, known by many as Ms. Elizabeth. She was a woman who always wore a different hat to church, along with her high

---

[20] Kitchin, George William, and Newbolt, Michael Robert, 1916, alt.; "Lift High the Cross." (c) 1974 Hope Publishing Company, Carol Stream, IL 60188. All rights reserved. Used by permission.

99

heels, and she would have already had a little discussion with you about your untucked flannel. She, along with her husband, Dick, was a member of Lovers Lane when Tom Shipp was pastor, and she was one of the most beloved members of the church of all time. She was set to turn ninety-seven years old a few days before she slipped away to feast at the Lord's Table in that heavenly banquet. Elizabeth was such a conduit of God's love, but she told me many times how overwhelmed she was with the acts of love shown to her by her "amazing church," as she put it. But the most poignant thing she ever told me was that she had "changed her mind on some matters."

Prior to me coming as her fourth pastor at Lovers Lane, Elizabeth cared lovingly for her husband the last ten years of his life while he battled Alzheimer's Disease. She loved all of the Lovers Lane pastors and was not shy to share her insights. All of us benefited from her friendship and faithfulness.

The last phone message I received from Elizabeth was after a sermon I preached on Christian family. It was a little "preachy" with some pointed directives. Someone told Elizabeth about the sermon. She called and left this message on my voicemail: "Love, I heard that you really laid it on 'em this morning. Go get 'em, tiger." *Click*. I really was not intending to "go get 'em," but after that call I strangely felt like growling.

One of the things that inspired me about Elizabeth was that she was always a learner. She loved to travel, mainly because she loved to learn.

She loved to see beautiful sites and places that she had read about all of her life. She especially loved seeing these sites with friends and loved learning in relationship. Elizabeth wanted to get everything she could out of every day that she was given.

About two years before she succumbed to the pancreatic cancer that she had bravely lived with for four years, she decided that she wanted to take the Alpha course. This is an eleven-week Christian short course that, at the time, about 1,000 of our members had taken and that eventually we would share with 8,000 women and men, who were incarcerated. The course is a two-hour weekly commitment to hear a lesson and then break into small groups for discussion. The class was at night, and her group was made up of mostly young adults. I asked her, what she was doing taking that evening Alpha course, and she said, "Son, you're never too old to learn, and I drive just fine at night." She loved that course and the young people she came to know and love.

Her group was very diverse, and two men in the group were a gay couple. I remember asking her about her group, and she said, "Son, I love them all. And God has taught me some things and has changed my mind about some matters." I didn't push that comment, but I, and others, witnessed her deepened faith and peaceful countenance that she attributed to her coursework with a group that had become very special to her.

Uplifting Crosses

When I just knew our time with her would only be weeks, I wanted to encourage her not to quit. "Give up" was not in her vocabulary and certainly not in her heart. Not only did she never quit, but she didn't want us to quit either. At the time, I was writing a book about my mentor, Bill Hinson, whom Elizabeth had met on a trip to the Passion Play in Oberammergau, Germany. Bill and Elizabeth became quick friends. Knowing that Elizabeth was ill, and thinking she probably would not see the book published, I took the manuscript over to her and told her that I was dedicating the book to her: "To Elizabeth Price, who epitomizes the love of Lovers Lane." She thanked me, gave me a little kiss, and she not only saw the book published in May 2006 but bought books for friends for the next two years. She wasn't finished; there was more that she had to do.

In the last months of Elizabeth's life, she seemed to be exiting with a heart full of thanksgiving. Though she had given so much of herself to the church, she wanted to do more. She commissioned some beautiful needlepoint kneelers that we enjoy today in the Shipp Chapel. She talked to me one day about wanting the new chapel to have a beautiful cross. She said that she had seen one that she wanted me to see and give my opinion. So one day I drove to her house in my Ford pickup, and she was "dressed to the nines," but not as formal as often she was. Let's just say her outfit fit in my truck and she was striking; she looked like Mrs. Barkley on the old western *The Big Valley*. We went to see the cross that had caught her eye.

The cross was at Highland Park Presbyterian Church and was crafted by a local artist, Barvo Walker. I loved this large and elegant altar cross. We then spent the day going from church to church, seeing crosses that she had identified. Then we talked to Barvo, who in two days gave us a rendering of a cross that today is in the Shipp Chapel and will bless us for years and years and years.

She wasn't finished. One day she called and said, "Son, the sanctuary needs a cross. Would you go over to Preston Hollow Presbyterian Church and see the gorgeous cross that is suspended in their sanctuary?" I said, "Elizabeth, what are you doing hanging out in all of these Presbyterian churches?" She said, "I don't know, son, but just go see the cross." I did, and the next thing you know the artist was at work on a masterpiece for our church.

During the thirty days that the sanctuary cross was being created, she slept a lot. I visited her on a Wednesday, and she said, "I am just going to rest in this bed until Sunday. Except for bridge on Friday night. You know that a lady will get off of her deathbed to get her hair done or play bridge." She was amazing.

In Elizabeth's last days, perhaps in part through Alpha and maybe even through her health challenge, she became real clear about the meaning of the cross. The cross became more and more beautiful to her, and she wanted us to have worship space that uplifted the cross. She lived life as one who followed her Lord of the cross, who knew her struggles and suffering in life. Yet her Lord was the Lord of the empty cross because he had risen and is alive. He was alive in her. The empty cross reminded her of the empty tomb, the full-to-overflowing promise of eternal life, and the feast at the Lord's Table at the heavenly banquet.

The End and the Beginning

The beautiful cross was finished, and it was striking. It stands simple and magnificent and reflects the colors of the stained glass throughout the sanctuary. In the center, where the crossbars meet, it has a crown of thorns that reminds us that our Lord suffered on a cross for our redemption. On Sunday, August 21, 2008, she got out of bed and put on one of her hundreds of classic Sunday hats and her highest of heels and stepped into the Lovers Lane pulpit for our 8:15, 9:30, and 11:00 worship services. She preached identically in each service without notes, saying,

> *"This Cross is presented to the glory of God and in appreciation for the prayers and tangible expressions of loving support from the clergy, staff, and laity of Lovers Lane United Methodist Church. I want us to have this cross in our gorgeous sanctuary. Thank you."*

After the last presentation, I led her to the back of the chancel and there were two young men there. Yes, they were the two gay men whom she loved and whom God used to "change her mind and her heart." One of the men said, "Pastor Stan, we're going to take her home." With that, he carefully swept her little eighty-pound, 97-year-old body up in his arms, walked her to their waiting automobile, and took her home. They put her in bed and made sure that she was comfortable and her caregivers were present. Elizabeth died a few days later.

Before she passed "over the Jordan" (an expression Bill Hinson used a lot), I visited Elizabeth one last time. She was in her bed and very weak. As lovingly as I could, I told her how blessed I was to call her friend and how many people loved her. Her last words to me in a hushed breath were "I hope I have done enough." I prayed with her, but I could almost hear the Lord whispering in the ear of this wonderful United Methodist Christian lady,

Elizabeth, it's enough. You've done plenty. Nothing has separated you from me. Nothing separates us now. You are home, and the heavenly banquet table is set. Your place is prepared for you among all of your sisters and brothers.

And Are We Yet Alive

By: Scott Gilliland

Okay, "Brother Copeland" (it feels weird to call you that, Stan), I never knew Elizabeth in this life, and yet through the retelling of her story in pulpits, at staff meetings, and in personal conversations, you have introduced her to the point that I'd swear I remember meeting her myself. What impresses me most about Elizabeth is the way she remained resolutely committed to two things till the end of her days, as far as I can tell.

First, I know enough to say Elizabeth was committed to Jesus. Even in her frail old age, she was finding ways to "lift high the cross" because she remembered something that is so easy for us to forget in the institutional church: The world needs the gospel of Jesus Christ. Not a gospel designed to bring us under a covenant of rules carefully edited, amended, and approved by two-third majority vote, but rather a gospel designed to bring us into relationship with the Christ it reveals. I know that my sisters and brothers who believe fervently in traditional concepts of marriage and sexuality do so not because they desire to bring pain or judgment on LGBTQ people, but because they have been led to this position through their living relationship with God in Christ. In the same way, I know that my sisters and brothers who believe fervently in full inclusion of LGBTQ persons in the life of the church do so not because they believe that culture outweighs the authority of Scripture, but because they have been led to this position through their living relationship with God in Christ. When I see the One Church Plan, I see a theology of church that believes in and trusts the individual's living relationship with Christ, and it removes those barriers that would prevent us from reaching all corners of the earth with the Good News that Jesus' love is for them.

Second, Elizabeth was committed to remaining teachable as long as she lived. She was excited to attend Alpha courses after decades of active life in the church. Even late into her nineties, she allowed her beliefs to be changed through her experiencing the care and love of two gay men in our congregation. The people I know who age most gracefully, and certainly those who get the most joy out of life, are those who remain teachable along the way.

I believe organizations are not any different; the best organizations are always open to learning, adapting, and rising to meet the needs of a new day, while those who adopt a rigid "we've always done it this way" mindset inevitably fade away as they grow obsolete. Can we learn from our history of schisms and mergers and realize that this argument over full inclusion will not be the final debate? By the time The United Methodist Church celebrates its one hundredth anniversary (God willing), we will most certainly have crossed bridges that we cannot even see at the present moment. If we are a teachable organization, then I believe we'll adopt the One Church Plan, a system better designed for organizing a global denomination in a fast-paced, dynamic twenty-first-century context.

In June 2018, I gathered with lay and clergy colleagues for the North Texas Annual Conference and sang a song that has quickly become familiar, even in the five short years I've been attending. "And Are We Yet Alive" serves as a poignant reminder for us as we begin our work each year. This year, however, the lyrics took on a different meaning for me. I sang them as one who was to be ordained roughly twenty-four hours later. I was about to join a covenant whose future is murky, nothing certain past February 2019. I was about to climb aboard what many believe to be a sinking ship. With these thoughts swimming in my head, I heard myself and the entire clergy session sing these words:

Let us take up the cross
till we the crown obtain,
and gladly reckon all things loss
so we may Jesus gain.[21]

"Gladly reckon all things loss." I think we ought to leave these words on the screens in future conferences, be they annual, jurisdictional, central, or general. Some Methodist voices promote a mentality that, in the future of United Methodism, there must be winners and losers . . . and Lord, no one wants to lose. We don't want to lose our arguments, our property, our pension, or our political influence. As a recovering know-it-all, I'm not sure of many things, but I'm very sure of this:

I want The United Methodist Church to lose.

I want us to lose the entrenched position we find ourselves in.

I want us to lose the wearied attitudes with which we meet our sisters and brothers every four years.

I want us to lose our pessimism that expects inaction and gridlock to rule the day.

I want us to lose our pride.

I want us to lose our self-righteousness.

---

[21] Charles Wesley, "And Are We Yet Alive," 1749, United Methodist Hymnal 1989, 553

I want us to lose our penchant to reduce others to labels.

I want us to lose the false dichotomy that plagues what should be nuanced discussions.

I want us to lose our love affair with legalism.

I want us to lose our distrust in each other.

I want us to lose our cynicism.

I want us to lose our fear.

I want us to lose anything that keeps us from uplifting the cross and proclaiming the gospel, so that the world (ourselves included) might gain Jesus.

The One Church Plan is not perfect. The United Methodist Church is not perfect. Lovers Lane is not perfect, nor is the church of anyone reading these words. But I see something in the One Church Plan that I know our denomination desperately needs if we hope to survive to see our centennial and beyond. The plan seeks to build trust. Trust in our local churches. Trust in our clergy and lay leadership. Trust in the living relationship with God in Christ.

As a young pastor who remains resolutely optimistic about this denomination that formed my faith, I pray we might lose ourselves these next months and years, and in so doing gain unity in our named essentials, grace in non-essentials, and trust that God is guiding us all, United Methodists all around the world.

Together

CHAPTER NINE
Breaking Up Is Hard to Do

By: Stan Copeland

An "Amicable" Separation?

As Neil Sedaka once said, "Breaking up is hard to do, *down doobie doo, down down, comma comma*." Many of us in the United Methodist Church find ourselves in the midst of what is, day by day, looking to be a breakup of sorts within our denomination, or an "amicable separation" as we have more politely talked about for years. Lately, I have had conversations with United Methodist friends and colleagues and have been taken aback by the realization that in coming months there is a chance that friendships will be different or mere memories of days gone by. This is all due to the distancing and plans for separation being calculated now. It hurts.

The mix of emotions, from sadness to anger, have arisen in me over the thought of friends and colleagues being like the Baptist brother down the street or the United Church of Christ sister up the street— fellow Christians but part of a different faith family. If truly a breakup occurs, we pastors will be Christian ministers, but we will no longer have the same surname, if you will—United Methodist. Our laity will share in Christian mission but without the sense of connection that once we had with other United Methodists.

113

My wife Tammy and I are pushing nearly forty years of marriage and thankfully divorce has never been discussed, though I think she may have thought of killing me a couple of times. Her parents and my parents have never experienced the pain of divorce either. But as a pastor, I have held the hands and whispered prayers with those devastated by the finality of divorce. We have all witnessed painful separation and the complications the children are forced to navigate.

Divorce is an excruciating reality for so many in our culture today, and the church percentages regarding divorce are as high as the general culture. The clergy statistics of those who are divorced have skyrocketed in the last four decades and are close to the national average. The Bible, with the words of Jesus, is not the initial tool that I use to comfort those who have made the decision that differences in the relationship are irreconcilable. We know that Jesus said this in Matthew's Gospel:

> *"It was also said, 'Whoever divorces his wife, let him give her a certificate of divorce.' But I say to you that anyone who divorces his wife, except on the grounds of unchastity, causes her to commit adultery; and whoever marries a divorced woman commits adultery."* (Matt 5:31-32)

The context for this passage centers around a culture where men could issue a divorce certificate too easily and then remarry at will. Jesus was addressing that context and raising the bar for his followers in the collection of passages that we call the Sermon on the Mount. Yet, on the matter of divorce and issues regarding other Levitical laws, including the way most of us choose to eat and what we choose to wear, we have made exceptions to what the Bible clearly mandates.

As Adam Hamilton points out in his book, *Making Sense of the Bible*, we certainly have moved away from the law of Moses regarding the sins that warrant the death penalty: sacrificing to a god other than Yahweh (Exod 22:20); persistent rebelliousness on the part of a child (Exod 21:18-21); a child who hits or curses her or his parents (Exod 21:15); working on the Sabbath (Exod 35:2); sexual intimacy when one partner is married to someone else (Lev 20:10); premarital sexual intercourse (Deut 22:13-21); and male homosexual sexual intimacy (Lev 20:13).[22]

A Discourse Headed for Divorce

On the eve of the Uniting Methodists' *Room for All* at Lovers Lane in the summer of 2018, I invited some colleagues over to our home for a discussion on the state of the church and the bishops' proposal to be addressed at the called General Conference in St. Louis in February 2019. The invitations went out to select United Methodists across the country. It felt like a blessing to be part of a connection that would allow me to have so many acquaintances from coast-to-coast. Not all

---

[22] Hamilton, A. (2014). *Making Sense of the Bible: Rediscovering the Power of Scripture Today.* NY, NY: HarperOne.

could attend, and I got the typical cordial regrets from some, but we still ended up having more than a houseful.

One response came back like a taste of bitter medicine. Knowing this colleague and experiencing him to be full of integrity, honesty, and straight-forwardness, I did not expect to receive the following reply:

> *Thanks for the invitation, Stan. I do not share your optimism about the One Church option. I will depart, and I expect my congregation will depart too, if the local option passes. No hard feelings. I simply don't want to be a part of the denomination you and the bishops envision.*

I wrote my friend back, and he responded very graciously, first apologizing for "venting," which was not offensive to me. Then he elaborated on his concerns with the bishops' One Church Plan. Furthermore, should the plan pass, he would work in his annual conference to encourage colleagues and congregations to leave. We shared a lengthy exchange of thoughts and opinions, a conversation I'm sure many have had with colleagues and friends as tensions have heightened in recent years.

As I sat reading one of his replies, I had tears in my eyes—not because I was convinced by his arguments, nor because he could not see my rationale as true. I had tears in my eyes due to a sense of loss. To think our denomination has allowed a debate on human sexuality to divide our mighty global church and most likely negatively impact our outreach to the world makes my heart sick. I realized that any additional response in writing would not be productive, so I deleted my drafted email, full of verbose counterpoints, and vowed to give him a call, until we can meet face to face.

I know that my colleague's sentiments are shared by many in our denomination, and that if any changes are made to our stance on same-sex marriage or ordination of LGBTQ persons, there are those prepared to organize a schism and leave.

As a part of developing this book, I wanted to sit down and talk with someone who understands what it means to be engaged in ministry in a more conservative or traditionalist setting, but who also sees contextual ministry as something to move toward, not away from.

Christian "Cowboy" Ethics

An Interview with Rev. Don Underwood, Christ UMC, Plano, TX

How many United Methodist pastors do you know who have a saddle in their office? Well, I know one, and he is one of a kind. The saddle is a show saddle of sorts, but he's had many saddles through the years and sat atop them wearing dusty jeans that didn't look like his daily, nicely pressed, clean ones he wore that day in his office. His signature white, starched dress shirt offset his tanned face, white hair, and mustache. Many United Methodists who are part of our General Conference delegations would know that I am describing the Reverend Don Underwood.

Don is as frustrated a cowboy as I am a farmer, and he gets up to his little spread of land about fifty minutes north of his church a few times a week to check on his horse and his cows. He has been an ordained United Methodist pastor for nearly five decades, but he's embraced a "cowboy ethic" right beside his strong Christian ethics as he has ridden high in the saddle at one of our largest churches, Christ United Methodist Church in Plano, Texas.

Whereas being a cowboy is in Don's heart, being a United Methodist pastor is in his genes. Don is a third-generation United Methodist pastor, and like his grandfather and father before him, has been a leader in our denomination. Don is a six-time North Texas Conference delegate to the General Conference. His grandfather was a General Conference delegate several times from the Memphis Conference and was also a delegate to the historic 1939 Uniting Conference in Kansas City, Missouri. Don's father, Bishop Walter Underwood, was also a delegate many times, including the historic Uniting Conference of 1968. In fact, for nine decades there has been a Don Underwood family clergy delegate to General Conference in the United Methodist Church. That has to be some sort of record that would put my friend and colleague in the United Methodist version of the *Guinness Book of World Records*.

I shared with Don some of the email exchange mentioned earlier in this chapter, and the deep sadness I felt about it. It was my need to seek his wisdom and offer his assessment of where the United

Methodist Church stands and what will the future General Conference do that brought me to set up time with him. I asked him first to share some of his General Conference experiences and memories.

Underwood: *I remember being a delegate to the General Conference in 2000 in Cleveland. During maybe the first plenary session, there was a lot of commotion and yelling and screaming, and we looked up and there was a woman sitting in the balcony not too far from me. She was threatening to jump. She was close enough that I contemplated whether some of us could catch her if she decided to jump, but she was high enough up that if she had have jumped she would have been seriously injured or killed. It was a startling moment, and I remember to this day what she was saying: "I'm a lesbian. I'm a lesbian. I've been a lesbian all of my life." Those of us who were there kind of see it as a divide and an eye-opener that this debate was going to get more and more heated.*

Four years later, in 2004 in Pittsburgh, I remember also running into a pastor friend from the Western Jurisdiction who was a General Conference delegate. He was a progressive and known in our connection as a great preacher and liberal theologian. He was highly respected for his intellect. We were discussing a push for gay marriage, and I raised the issue that if we accept gay marriage then that would satisfy the fidelity in marriage mandate for gay and lesbian persons. The pressing question of our conversation was "and then what will we do?" He said, with confidence, "That will never happen." And we were both wrong. Culture has changed. The Supreme Court decision was a watershed moment in our country and for the gay and lesbian movement.

Copeland: What about in your congregation? Is same-sex marriage a hot-button issue?

Underwood: *My congregation is diverse in beliefs on same-sex marriage, but we are clear and united on the fact that our doors, minds, and hearts are open. We have tried to emphasize that what unites us as United Methodists is greater than the many issues that divide us, human sexuality being one of them. It is becoming more of a topic of conversation in my congregation since the Supreme Court decision. The decision to legalize [same-sex] marriage changed the culture, and the culture always impacts the church. If that weren't the case, we'd still be riding horses between our charges, there would be no women clergy, and there would be few, if any, divorced persons in our churches. It is naïve to say the church never follows the culture. The church always has to decide which parts of the culture it will follow and which part it's not going to follow, and that is really where we find ourselves today.*

Cultural shifts happen first, and then the church adapts to those shifts or rejects them. When Galileo was finally vindicated, the church accepted a post-Copernican cosmology that Galileo championed. The church said, "Okay, so the earth is not the center of the universe, and in fact we believe with Galileo and Copernicus before him that the sun is the universe's center." The cultural shift in physics was made, and the church chose to accept it after fighting for years and struggling with the crisis of faith regarding the Bible that supported a different cosmology. The church generally follows major cultural shifts, and to say otherwise is ridiculous.

We are seeing changing attitudes among many Americans on the issues related to homosexuality. I think where this has made a difference in our church is that people are much more open about their sexuality. Likewise, younger generations are at a different place on these issues by and large, and business people who run corporations have long since made the shift to a more accepting environment. For these and many others, this is an old debate. We have gay and lesbian couples in our church and some have children. And we baptize these children without thinking twice about it. When I came home from General Conference in Fort Worth in 2008, about two weeks afterward, a lesbian couple came to me requesting that I baptize their baby. They stood before the congregation and our people knew this was a lesbian couple. I baptized the baby and did not hear one word of protest. That made me feel so good about the love that characterizes our church.

Our church is diverse, but our county—Collin—is arguably one of the most conservative counties in the country. Christ Church may be more moderate than our general public in Collin County, but we are generally conservative. I addressed our largest Sunday School class a few years ago and it is a diverse class age-wise and in every other way. The format was "question the preacher on any matter," and homosexuality came up. So, I told them that if the church ever wants same-sex marriage, one way or the other, to be a main issue at Christ Church, they would need to ask for another pastor. This is an important issue, but it has never been what animates my ministry or motivates my mission and vision of the church.

I have said for some time now that our laypeople have taught me a lot and shown me how to deal with this matter. In this class of mature adults, one set of friends disagree on this subject and gather week after week in class. They will go out to eat with each other and play bridge with one another, all the time disagreeing on matters pertaining to homosexuality. Both know that one has a gay grandson that has come out, and he has changed their minds on these matters. They set aside their differences and positions out of respect for the other and just don't talk about it. They still come to church together, go to Sunday School together, recreate together; they just don't think it is important enough to split up their friendship. So, to me, our laypeople have shown us how we can stay together in the life of the church. For those who elevate this to an ultimate or a penultimate level, on the right and the left, it just doesn't work for them. For most of us, we would say this is an important matter that needs to be dealt with theologically, and in the church, but it is not an ultimate or penultimate matter. It is in no way unimportant to me, and I am not trying to be cavalier about the feelings of those who are on the right and left, but from a theological and missional perspective it is not an essential for me, and I believe that is the case for many.

Copeland: Can you say a word about the contextualization uplifted in the One Church Plan option?

Underwood: *One reason I support the One Church option over the others is that it is contextual and lends itself to more local autonomy. It is also really interesting to see the support coming out of the Council of Bishops and their affirmation of contextualization. For the bishops, of all people, to endorse more local autonomy shows that it is really the only good option we have if we are going to stay together as a denomination. We are so diverse that if we don't move toward more local control, or local autonomy, then there is no way we can hold it together. The fact that the Council of Bishops recognizes this, and it is not particularly in their self-interest, is of particular importance, and everybody should take notice. If you consider what contextualization means, it gives more control to the local church and less importance to the General Conference, the bishops, and the agencies.*

From my perspective, as a large church pastor, I have wanted contextualization for years. We've wanted more local control. All of us who have grown large churches have done so more in spite of the Discipline, not with the help of the Discipline. We have ignored parts of the Discipline in order to craft our ministry in a way that makes sense in our settings, our mission fields.

It is possible with contextualization that we are going to see the dissolution of a lot that we have seen as unmovable for a long time. The African delegates have been trying to lead us to a place of more mission focus and away from matters that they say they have little interest in. The plan going forward that does the least to upset to the flow of mission funding will be important to all of our Central Conferences. Our African delegation is not monolithic and will be looking for the plan that is the "do no harm" plan or the least amount of harm. Passing the One Church Plan moves the debates related to human sexuality off center stage and subordinates it to other missional priorities, and that will be welcomed by most Central Conference delegates.

Another reason the One Church option works is that it reflects the messiness of the way things are right now. The One Church option acknowledges and defines where we are in this particular moment. I hope we will pass it and move forward to a new day where we can prioritize making disciples, transforming lives, and creating the kingdom of God on earth.

Copeland: What about those who say they cannot stay in our denomination if the One Church Plan passes?

Underwood: *I know there are some people who have utter clarity that they will start another denomination if One Church passes. There are those who have envisioned another Wesleyan expression for some time now. There is no doubt in my mind that there are churches and there are coalitions that are planning a new denomination of some kind if the General Conference does not vote to retain the traditional position on homosexuality.*

None of the proposals of A Way Forward are perfect solutions. I support the One Church model for several reasons, but I am concerned about getting anything passed if the General Conference displays the same kind of dysfunction it did the first few days in Portland in 2016. However, I am not anxious about any of this because General Conference has become more and more irrelevant. It will be so until we shift the focus to mission that we largely agree upon and subordinate the discussion of largely United States–concerns and politically charged social agenda to that primary mission of the church.

Later that day, I listened to a sermon Don had preached on Acts 15 that I thought was brilliant, and I asked if he had written anything on the subject of where the church is at this point in time regarding human sexuality. He shared this article (which will close the chapter) entitled, "The Acts 15 Question: An Evangelical Perspective."

The Acts 15 Question: An Evangelical Perspective
By: Don Underwood

The United Methodist Church has been struggling with the issue of human sexuality for almost five decades, specifically around the questions of ordination and same-gender marriage. The polity debate has centered primarily around several pivotal passages in the Book of Discipline. Among them is paragraph 161(G) in the Social Principles, which reads, in part: "The United Methodist Church does not condone the practice of homosexuality and considers this practice incompatible with Christian teaching. We affirm that God's grace is available to all. We will seek to live together in Christian community, welcoming, forgiving, and loving one another, as Christ has loved and accepted us. We implore families and churches not to reject or condemn lesbian and gay members and friends. We commit ourselves to be in ministry for and with all persons."

Paragraph 304.3, dealing with qualifications for ordination, says, "The practice of homosexuality is incompatible with Christian teaching. Therefore, self-avowed practicing homosexuals are not to be certified as candidates, ordained as ministers, or appointed to serve in The United Methodist Church."

Paragraph 304.2 delineates the requirements for holy living of ordained ministers: ". . . To this end, they agree to exercise responsible self-control by personal habits conducive to bodily health, mental and emotional maturity, integrity in all personal relationships, fidelity in marriage and celibacy in singleness, social responsibility, and growth in grace and in the knowledge and love of God."

These passages and others have been challenged repeatedly, but the General Conference has consistently voted not to delete or change them.

As the special called General Conference approaches, there is renewed interest in whether there is a traditional/conservative theological and biblical approach that justifies changes to the Book of Discipline. The quandary of accepting baptized LGBTQ persons as brothers and sisters in Christ while denying them access to the gifts of marriage and ordained ministry impacts progressives and traditionalists alike. How do we state that we fully accept LGBTQ persons as brothers and sisters in Christ while denying them full inclusion as ordained clergy and full acceptance as faithful marriage partners? The changing cultural landscape in which that question is being engaged now includes the fact that same-sex marriage has been ruled legal by both courts and civil legislative bodies—not only in the United States but also in many countries worldwide—and is increasingly affirmed by people in general. According to the Pew Research Center, 63 percent of Americans said in 2016 that homosexuality should be accepted by society, compared with 51 percent in 2006.[23] That trajectory has been consistent and shows no signs of reversal as more and more Americans self-identify as LGBTQ.

---

[23] Source: Pew Research Center, Survey conducted April 12-19, 2016

Acts 15

The narrative of Acts 10–15, which relates the early church's struggle with the acceptance of Gentiles, has been widely read and discussed by scholars, clergy, and laypeople as an example of how the church dealt with a changing culture. Both challenges and opportunities were presented to the young church by the fact that Gentiles were enthusiastically converting to Christianity. The question of circumcision, which was a requirement of Hebraic law, was especially salient in the debate. Conservative members of the church were (reluctantly) moving toward acceptance of Gentiles, but with the caveat that they first be circumcised in accordance with Hebrew law and tradition. Other apostles, including Paul, Peter, and Barnabas, argued for full acceptance without imposition of ritual circumcision. Ultimately, the elders at the Jerusalem Council issued this decree in welcoming uncircumcised Gentiles as followers of Jesus: **"The Holy Spirit has led us to the decision that no burden should be placed on you other than these essentials: refuse food offered to idols, blood, the meat from strangled animals, and sexual immorality. You will do well to avoid such things. Farewell."** (Acts 15: 28-29 CEB)

While Acts 15 has been widely discussed as an example of how the church made the decision to be radically inclusive, too little attention has been given to the specific remedy provided in the above reference. The requirement of circumcision was deemed to be not only a "burden," but an unessential requirement for faithful discipleship. In their statement, the apostles created clarity about the "essential" requirements for discipleship. Although admittedly archaic by today's standards, they not only distinguished them from ritual circumcision, but also laid the foundation for what they deemed to be faithful living within the confines of Christian community. In other words, the exclusion of the requirement for circumcision did not mean withdrawal from a commitment to mutually agreed upon standards of Christian conduct. They managed to thread the needle that would allow greater inclusion without opening the door so wide that there would be license for moral anarchy.

The Jerusalem Council example presents the opportunity to ask three questions that might guide the debate about how to move forward on the debates surrounding human sexuality:

Question 1:

Was the solution of the Jerusalem Council driven primarily by a move toward a loosening of accepted codes of conduct, or by an evangelical commitment to grow the kingdom of God? The reports of the apostles about the enthusiastic discipleship of Gentile converts would suggest the latter. It could be argued that "inclusion" was not the pivotal motivation, but rather a radical evangelistic vision about the kingdom of God, which had been vividly described by Jesus in numerous teachings. From this perspective, the contemporary categories of "progressive" and "traditional" seem inappropriate. Perhaps the shared commitment to the Great Commandment provides a more appropriate rationale for understanding the decision.

Question 2:

Is it possible that, in today's contemporary debate, the requirement for celibacy from faithful, same-gender married partners is analogous to the "burden" of the requirement for circumcision? Can we claim to fully accept gay and lesbian brothers and sisters while imposing upon them a "burden" of celibacy that is otherwise unacceptable in Protestant tradition? This question is, admittedly, impacted by cultural changes that could hardly have been anticipated a generation ago. Typical gay couples sitting in United Methodist pews today are more likely to be carrying diaper bags than placards pleading for sexual liberation. Many of them are traditional/conservative in their political, ideological, and theological beliefs. Is our current understanding of the complexities of human sexuality leading us to a deeper and richer understanding of how persons can love one another within the covenantal bounds of marriage? If so, is it possible for the church to expand the "essentials" of "celibacy in singleness and fidelity in marriage" to include those who self-identify in ways that are not traditionally heterosexual? If so, this would meet even the "essentials" test of Acts 15.

Question 3:

Is it possible that a reorientation of our evangelistic vision will reach generations that currently consider the church's view of human sexuality to be narrow at best, bigoted at worst, and clearly hypocritical? Peter's argument that **"we and they are saved in the same way, by the grace of the Lord Jesus"** (Acts 15:11) is a uniting statement, but also a confessional statement, based upon our common humanity. It can be argued, without denigrating the importance of it, that the ongoing debate over human sexuality has sapped our energy, diverted us from important ministry and mission, and compromised our vision. By putting this debate behind us, might we unleash a new evangelistic passion and reach new generations who have been turned off because of this debate? Regardless of theological orientation, what true United Methodist does not yearn for a return to truly passionate witness, service, and ministry?

Conclusion:

Much is at stake in the church's current debate about human sexuality. Traditionalists and evangelicals are rightly concerned about a movement to an *ecclesia* that has no stated standards for what constitutes a Christian lifestyle. But Acts 10–15, and specifically the solution of the Jerusalem Council, offers a biblical vision for how the church could radically expand its understanding and mission without sacrificing the essentials of faithful discipleship. Could it be that, in our current debate about human sexuality, God is calling us to a richer and deeper understanding about what it means to be the body of Christ? Is it possible that this is an Acts 15 moment, and that the Holy Spirit brought us to this place?

Together

EPILOGUE
Two Final Words

Foolish Expectations

By: Scott Gilliland

I'm a recovering cynic.

Some people are addicted to alcohol. Some are addicted to drugs. Some are addicted to shopping, or eating, or sex, but I'm addicted to cynicism.

Nothing feels better than being comfortably certain that everything stinks and nothing will ever get better. To adopt the smug smile of one who really "gets it" while everyone else foolishly clings to false hope. And I'm far from the only one.

Because the honest truth is not only does it feel good to be cynical, it's also really easy. Anyone who observes the world in which we live for more than a millisecond can figure out that evil and brokenness are pervasive, even overwhelming. All the cynic has to do is sit back and say, "It'll never change." And not only does that feel good, but it's easy too, because when you're certain nothing will ever change, then you don't even have to try.

As we have lived in the liminal space between General Conferences of 2016 and 2019, I imagine you're like me and you've heard a lot of

133

cynicism from your colleagues and friends—and maybe from yourself as well.

"What's really going to be different this time?"
"We all know a split will happen eventually."
"This is just like what happened to the Presbyterians and Episcopalians."
"We're just wasting our time."

These are thoughts I have heard dozens of times over, and they're thoughts that have found a home in my own head at times, too. What about you?

I consider it a blessing to serve at Lovers Lane, where we have a robust recovery ministry space called The Center for Spiritual Development, home to what we think is the largest Twelfth Step Ministry in the country, with almost one hundred groups meeting there weekly for any addiction you can imagine. (One of their leaders, who is a member at our church, likes to say "If you have an 'ism,' we have a 'wasm'!") I have learned from my friends in recovery that you never stop being in recovery; once you are in recovery for your addiction, you are in recovery for life.

And I am a recovering cynic.

I am addicted to the smug smile and the "know-it-all" posture. I am addicted to the laziness disguised as intelligence and the ignorance disguised as certainty. I am addicted to never having to put myself at risk for anything, since I've determined it will fail before I even try.

I am in recovery. For life.

We like to tease optimists as "naïve" or "Bambi-types," because it can be hard to hear that the sun will rise when we are caught in a thunderstorm at night. But I think that optimists might just be the bravest, strongest people in the world.

When you are an optimist, you have a dream worth working toward, foolish as that dream might be. Some of the most foolish dreams have made our world a significantly better place.

Imagine if Martin Luther King Jr. had tempered his dreams with cynicism? Or Nelson Mandela? Or Susan B. Anthony? Or John Wesley? Or even Jesus?

It could be said that in today's political climate, in our culture of divisiveness, the dream of fighting to stay together is a foolish one.

It is foolish to dream that temple-minded Christians could worship with their tabernacle-minded counterparts.

It is foolish to dream that liberals, conservatives, and independents could submit their ideologies to a common cross.

It is foolish to dream that an institutional denomination with roots hundreds of years old could offer a relevant message to a generation fed up with organized religion.

It is foolish to dream that our decline in American membership could be a season of revival waiting to happen, if only we could regain a passion for the mission of our church.

It is foolish to dream that the Holy Spirit could actually be using this tension-filled season to bring about a clarifying vision of The United Methodist Church in the twenty-first century.

It is foolish to dream that in the midst of our bureaucratic infighting, lives are still being touched and transformed by the grace of God every single moment of every single day, even when we fail.

It is foolish to dream that the best days of The United Methodist Church are not behind us, but ahead of us.

It's absolutely foolish.

Which is why this recovering cynic has to believe it's worth fighting for. It's worth risking myself and my pride. It's worth being teased as an optimist. It's worth feeling like a fool, hoping and praying God shows up in a recklessly redemptive way.

My introduction to ministry was at my home church following college. I showed up ready to follow what I was sure was God's call on my life, bright-eyed and bushy-tailed, like the Disney-movie deer we know. What I did not expect was eighteen months of difficult ministry in a church going through a painful "dying" season during the fallout of the 2008 financial crisis. The adults who had helped shape and mold me in my faith as a child were now revealing themselves to be thoroughly human, and it was a bitter pill to swallow. I eventually left that position without another job to fall back upon and moved back in with my parents. Living the dream of every twenty-two-year-old.

I had resolved to never trust the church again, to never work in an institution I deemed too broken to give my life to. But after months of unemployment in a brutal job market, I was desperate. I sat in my room—technically my parents' guest room since I had moved out years before—and in total darkness I did something I had not done for months or maybe even a year.

I prayed.

I prayed the prayer of a twenty-two-year old who was broken and had bills to pay, "God, I thought you called me to ministry before, and even though I'm not sure I trust you completely, if you'll just give me something—anything—I'll do it."

(It should be said that as a recovering cynic, I hate cheesy testimonies. It should also be said that I believe God has a very real sense of humor, because God gave me a cheesy testimony.)

That same night, at just past midnight, I received a Facebook message from a former co-worker, Jamie, who was at that time working at Lovers Lane. The message read, "I heard you are on the job market, and I want to talk to you about coming to work with me in the Kids Ministry!"

When I walked into Lovers Lane for the first time about a week or so later, I'm sure my cynical self was certain what I would find: another broken church with broken people who would break me again.

Did I expect to meet Raegan?
Did I expect to be married to Raegan within the year?
Did I expect my faith to be resurrected?
Did I expect to start seminary within two years?
Did I expect to follow a call to ordained ministry?
Did I expect to not only have a daughter, but to have her baptized by the senior pastor I was about to meet?

My expectation was to be let down in every single way, because the pain in my life had taught me to be a cynic. Thankfully, that night in my parents' guest room, as I prayed a desperate prayer, God set me on a path of recovery by proving to be full of surprises in a life that I never could have seen coming.

Maybe you expect 2019 to let you down because the pain of past conferences has taught you to be a cynic. I hope you will join me in recovery. Because the church does not need more cynics, and cynicism will not build the kingdom of our foolishly optimistic God. I pray we can resurrect a spirit of optimism—born of prayer and even desperation—in our denomination, because foolish dreams are worth fighting for, and we are so much stronger as optimistic fools together than we will be as cynics apart.

A Gift of Hope from a Shoe-Shining Angel

By: Stan Copeland

Let me share a story with you regarding a General Conference experience that gives me hope. In February 2019, the United Methodist General Conference will be called together for three days to deal with the Council of Bishops' recommended One Church Plan alongside the other two proposals put forth by the Commission on a Way Forward. For months I have been pondering the question "Can any good thing come out of a United Methodist General Conference?" General Conferences for decades seem to be becoming more and more contentious and dysfunctional. There is no question that no good will come out of General Conference apart from the Holy Spirit leading us to the living water of unity in Christ, and all of us drinking deeply without fear or cynicism. The world is being led by so many false prophets to stagnant pools of division and hate. Will The United Methodist Church rise above our differences in our eclectic family and seize the day to echo the words of our Lord: "We offer you the living water of Jesus's love that has the power to cast out fear."

Every once in a while, I have the feeling that I am in the presence of an angel. By "angel" I mean a messenger from God who has just come my way and offers a clarifying word that is unmistakably from God and exactly the directing instruction I long to hear.

I met such a spiritual messenger at the 2004 General Conference, which is infamously one of our most conflict-ridden United Methodist gatherings ever. It was my first time to be a delegate to General Conference, though I had previously been an alternate to the General Conference from the Texas Conference. I was now a delegate from the North Texas Conference. The Conference had been going on for days, and there was jockeying for political advantages and arguing positions with little evidence of Holy Conferencing or respectfully listening to one another. I was weary and in a hurry to get from the hotel to the Convention Center when I met the angel.

He had no wings, no harp, no halo. He was a large African-American man who appeared to be in his sixties, shining shoes at his shoe-shine station at the hotel. I was in a hurry, but I recognized the man in the chair getting his shoes shined. I walked over and greeted my friend with a handshake above the bent-over shoe-shine man who was steady at his task. Without looking up, and no doubt looking down at my shoes, he said, "You sure need a shine." I looked down and he was right, I needed a shine. I immediately thought of the fact that I would soon see my mentor, Bill Hinson, at the Convention Center. He always noticed a preacher's shoes, and he would certainly examine mine. I replied, "You're surely right. Could I be next in your chair if I get a quick cup of coffee over there and come right back?" The man never looked up as he said, "Sure, you can be next. That is if somebody don't come up before you get back." I didn't know yet that I was in the presence of an angel, but I knew I was dealing with a character. Forget the coffee. I wanted to know more about this man.

I must admit when I climbed in his chair I was fairly cynical about the work of the General Conference and wondered whether this man with the shine brushes would add to my frustrations. Shortly into the art of his trade of making my black wingtips come back to life, I noticed a large scar on his neck. No doubt he had been asked dozens of times, "How'd you get that scar?" and the story couldn't be a good one. It was probably a good choice not to ask.

To the rhythm of his brushstrokes he continued to gaze on my shoes as he said, "You with the Methodists?" I said, "Yes, sir." Still not looking up from his rhythm of brushing that he must find himself in all day long, he said, "How's it going over there?" I said, "Not too well. It seems that we haven't gotten to the main thing yet. It seems all we are doing is fighting over language and beliefs related to controversial social issues." He stopped brushing, picked up his polish, and looked me in the eye, saying, "You know the main thing, don't you? It's Jesus. You know who Jesus is? He's the main thing." He probably assumed I was a preacher, but he may not have known he was an angel.

He went back to his work, but he was fully engaged with me now, looking up into my eyes and then down to the shoes as he continued, "Only Jesus could have taken me from where I was to where I am today." He said, "I was an angry man. I hated everybody, especially white folk." He put down the polish, having completed the more tedious, polishing task. He picked up his buffing rag and said, "And you know what Jesus taught me? He taught me that I had to love ME, before I could love HIM, or before I could really love anybody else." He continued to buff. "Jesus taught me that he loved me enough to die on a cross for me, and if he loved me that much the least I could do is love me. Now, that is called grace. And it's God's love—a gift for ALL people. Even those people carrying those signs and protesting out there. You gotta love 'em."

He looked up with the buffing rag in hand and the word of the Holy Spirit on his lips. "Now I love me and I even love you and I don't even know you. And I sure love Jesus. He saved my life. I put my faith in him. He's never let me down. I put my faith in him every day. I wake up and say, 'God, thank you for another day to love you, love all the people I'll see today, and love me too.' I put my faith in him every day."

With that, he started buffing again. He was finishing up, but the time was no longer an issue for me, as my hurried state had calmed. Then he popped the rag and said, "Done, sir." I expected the next words out of his mouth to be, "That will be five dollars." Instead he said, "Let me pray with you." He put his big arm on my shoulder and said, "Jesus, lift my brother's spirits and have him go across the street, over there to the Methodists, and tell 'em about the main thing." What a shoeshine! I tipped him $5 and I should have tipped him $500. I extended my hand and his big hand gripped mine. I said, "Thanks, brother. I needed that shine more than my shoes did."

I got out of his chair, but I was not the same person who sat down in it. I was lighter, freer, reminded of the real purpose: "Making disciples of 'the Main Thing' (Jesus Christ) for the transformation of the world." I walked across the street in my shiny wingtips, ready to face the General Conference, and I started whistling a song that just came right out of my heart.

I once said about General Conference 2004 that "It would be trite to say it was 'another verse of the same old song' that had been sung for decades. It would be more accurate to say the General Conference was many different songs being sung at once with some singers trying hard to be heard over others, and particularly over the mainstream choir."[24] How I long for a sacred harmony of United Methodists singing different notes or even the kind of coming together like the notes of dissonance in bluesy gospel, but the point is we sing together, and together we United Methodists can make beautiful, missional music.

[24] Copeland, S. R. (2006). *Lord, He Went: Remembering William H. Hinson.* Nashville: Abingdon Press.

The song on my lips, as I left the shoe-shining angel, I sometimes call the United Methodist National Anthem.

O for a thousand tongues to sing
My great Redeemer's praise,
the glories of my God and King,
the triumphs of his days.

My gracious Master and my God,
assist me to proclaim,
to spread through all the earth abroad
the honors of thy name.

Jesus the name that charms our fears,
that bids our sorrows cease;
'tis music in the sinner's ears,
'tis life, and health and peace.

He breaks the power of canceled sin,
he sets the prisoner free;
his blood can make the foulest clean;
his blood availed for me.

He speaks and listening to His voice
new life the dead receive;
the mournful, broken hearts rejoice,
the humble poor believe.[25]

---

[25] Charles Wesley, "O For a Thousand Tongues to Sing," 1739, United Methodist Hymnal 1989, 57

APPENDIX

Lovers Lane Mission Statement

Loving ALL people into relationship with Jesus Christ.

Lovers Lane Vision Statement

One diverse community, passionately engaging the Bible, uplifting Jesus in worship and loving service, and challenging in Love that which divides.

Lovers Lane Dream Statement

By God's grace,

following the Resurrected Lord

and empowered by the Holy Spirit

we dream that with humility, courage, and authenticity

we will . . .

worship God in multiple, dynamic venues across the Metroplex,

baptize as an experience of God's unconditional love,

engage the Bible in hundreds of classes & groups,

become a sacred harmony of thousands of God's children,

serve tens-of-thousands with an "ALL are precious in His sight" passion,

and Love ALL people into relationship with Jesus Christ.

Together